THE AUDITOR

AN
INSTRUCTIONAL NOVELLA

BY

JAMES K. LOEBBECKE

Kenneth A. Sorensen
Peat Marwick Professor of Accounting
University of Utah

Prentice Hall, Upper Saddle River, New Jersey 07458

Dedicated, in memoriam, *to*

Thomas Jefferson Ennis
Milton M. Gilmore
W. Donald Georgen

No young auditor could have hoped
to work for three finer
professionals or human beings.

Executive Editor: Annie Todd
Editorial Assistant: Elaine Oyzon-Mast
Production Editor Lynda Paolucci
Managing Editor: Bruce Kaplan
Manufacturing Buyer: Lisa DiMaulo
Senior Manufacturing Supervisor: Paul Smolenski
Manufacturing Manager: Vincent Scelta
Cover Design: Bruce Kenselaar
Art Director: Jayne Conte
Composition: Pine Tree Composition, Inc.

Copyright ©1999 by Prentice-Hall, Inc.
A Simon & Schuster Company
Upper Saddle River, New Jersey 07458

Loebbecke, James K.
    The Auditor : an instructional novella / by James K. Loebbecke.
        p.   cm.
    ISBN 0–13–079976–9 (alk. paper)
        1. Accountants—Fiction. 2. Auditing—Fiction. I. Title.
    PS3562.034A9   1999
    813′.54—dc21   98–5808
                                                                     CIP

Prentice-Hall International (UK) Limited, *London*
Prentice-Hall of Australia Pty. Limited, *Sydney*
Prentice-Hall Canada, Inc., *Toronto*
Prentice-Hall Hispanoamericana, S.A., *Mexico*
Prentice-Hall of India Private Limited, *New Delhi*
Prentice-Hall of Japan, Inc., *Tokyo*
Simon & Schuster Asia Pte. Ltd., *Singapore*
Editora Prentice-Hall do Brasil, Ltda., *Rio De Janeiro*

Printed in the United States of America
10 9 8 7 6 5 4

Contents

Preface

It is often said that a difficulty in teaching auditing is that it seems very abstract to students in the classroom. Auditing texts focus, as they should, on concepts and standards. Students do exercises and practice sets, but these rarely represent the audit work experience in any real way. Some taste of practice is often provided through guest speakers and use of video and computer-based educational programs. But these still may not be enough to satisfy students' natural curiosity about the field they may enter upon graduation; and they may not provide much help in career planning.

The purpose of *The Auditor* is to add to the teaching tools that provide students with insight into actual audit practice. It tells the story of Jack Butler, a man from the San Francisco Bay area who goes to Farwestern State University, majors in accounting, and goes to work for the Oakland office of The Firm, a large public accounting firm. Over the course of the book, the events of Jack's career, and the careers of a number of his colleagues, unfold. These events deal with various aspects of a career in public accounting that students should know about and be prepared for as they make the transition from academia to practice. Many of the events also serve to emphasize the relative importance of conventional lessons that the students have learned in school.

The book is divided into fourteen short chapters that deal with logical events or sets of events over Jack Butler's career, from recruiting to partnership, although not necessarily in chronological order. Each of the chapters can be assigned so that they are spread evenly over a semester or quarter period, requiring only a few minutes of reading each week. Many of the technical topics will coincide with the timing of conventional text materials.

Thus, *The Auditor* is intended to be used as supplemental reading in an auditing class. It can be used in basic auditing or advanced auditing classes. The difference will be in the extent and depth of the discussions that will be held. In basic auditing, where time is generally at a premium, students can be asked simply to read *The Auditor* out of class, and a select number of the discussion questions provided at the end of each chapter can be designated for class discussion. In an advanced auditing class, a great deal more elaboration and in-depth discussion can take place. It would also be feasible to use the book in both levels of instruction for the same students. At the basic level they would be introduced to practical aspects, and then they would go back and discuss them in depth in later, fifth-year classes.[1]

Also, the telling of Jack's story is flavored with "Bearisms," short rules of thumb that emanate from Quentin Barnes, the partner in charge of Jack's office. These Bearisms are listed in an appendix at the end of the book and also can be used as discussion points in various ways in the auditing classroom. For example, one instructor I know starts each class with a "saying of the day" based on the Bearisms.

In reading *The Auditor,* it is important to understand that the characters, The Firm and its clients, Farwestern State University, and the events described are fictional and not intended to portray real persons, organizations, or events. Also, the book does not intend to present *all* of the aspects of public accounting that one will encounter. However, the book is representative of relevant personalities and experiences that one might encounter in a typical career with a large or, for that matter, small public accounting firm.

Finally, I'd like to thank Kristin Loebbecke for the tremendous assistance she provided as editor of this book. Her suggestions, corrections, and encouragement were invaluable.

J.K.L.

---

[1]One reviewer of the book suggested that the first seven chapters could be read in the first intermediate accounting course as a basis for discussing career planning, with the last seven chapters being read in the auditing class.

1

The Big Day

L ast night was miserable. I tossed and turned and went over a thousand times my thoughts about what might happen today. The last time I had a night like this was when my daughter, Jenny, had pneumonia and had to spend the night in the hospital. Libby didn't seem to notice my anxiety. Every time I rolled over, she seemed to be sleeping peacefully. When morning finally came and I showered, got dressed, and came down to breakfast, Libby was as bright and cheery as ever.

"Hi, honey! Ready for bacon and eggs?"

"I really couldn't eat anything right now, Lib. All I can think about is getting to the office."

Libby gave me one of her mother-to-child stares. "I know this is a big day for you, Jack. You ought to start it off right. Sit down and relax for a few minutes. Read the paper and eat. You told me you had this whole thing under control, didn't you?"

"Yeah, but I lied."

I was anxious; actually, more than that. I had worked in the Oakland office of The Firm ever since I graduated from Farwestern State University almost ten years ago. I am one of three managers who are being considered for partnership, and today I'll find out if I'm in. Quentin Barnes, the partner in charge of our office, is on The Firm's policy board. He went to New York to meet with the board on Friday and Saturday, where they made the final new-partner cut. Quentin will be back in the office this morning with the results of the meeting.

The other two candidates are Don Parnell and Barb Gillespie. We are all close friends and rooting for one another. The reality, however, is that probably only one of us, perhaps two, will make it. The Firm's managing partner knows that his success is largely based on whether earnings per partner go up each year. One way to make that happen is to increase overall earnings. The other way is to keep the number of partners down. This means that the decision to make new partners is a very careful one. The board looks at all candidates through a magnifying glass and debates their strengths and weaknesses endlessly. It helps to have a strong mentor like Quentin Barnes to support you at the meeting.

Most of my thoughts during the night had been about each of our chances of being accepted into The Firm. Don and I are audit managers, and Barb is a tax manager. Don is an outstanding technician, better than I am—but I'm pretty good. I'm better with clients and practice development. Barb is outstanding in every way. And she's been with The Firm for a year longer than Don and I have. Finally, the office can absorb only one new partner in the audit department. Whether there's room for another partner in the tax department is hard for me to say. It probably depends on whether Roy Shantz, the partner in charge of the department, decides to retire this year or next.

In my semi-awake state, I imagined myself in Barnes's office. First, he would tell me that I am on the list and I would feel elated. Then I would go through it again and he would say, "Sorry, Jack, it just didn't happen for you this time out," and I would feel depressed. In another very contorted version, Barnes would call both Don and me into his office and tell us to arm wrestle: The winner would get promoted, and the loser would have to spend the rest of his career in the mail room. After that, I rolled over and sighed to myself, "What's the big deal, Jack? If you make it, you make it. If you don't, you don't. What's so important about becoming a partner anyway?"

What *is* so important about becoming a partner? The more I thought about this, the more I realized that after nine and a half years of working for The Firm, I was having a hard time separating myself as a person from myself as a professional. I am a husband, a father, a son, a brother, a friend, and many other things. But so much of my effort and direction has been toward achieving success in The Firm, and, let's face it, that means becoming a partner. If I make it, particularly by the ten-year mark, it will validate me as a person, won't it? And if I don't, does it mean that I failed—or that I'm a failure?

Libby and I have discussed this many times. Libby is the rock of the family. Before Jon and Jenny were born, Libby was an elementary school teacher. She is the oldest of four kids, and because both her parents worked in her father's business, she played a major role in looking after her younger brother and sisters. She is the crisis master, the caregiver. She has the patience of Job but has a hard time understanding why this promotion seems almost like life or death to me. She has told me many times that she would be very happy with the status and money the promotion will bring, but it's not going to make *her* life a success or failure. But she also has great confidence in me and believes that I am a shoe-in.

With some of Libby's confidence rubbing off on me and a cup of coffee starting to burn a hole in my stomach, I began the twenty-minute drive down the hill to the office. My last glance was of Libby looking out the front door, giving me a smile and holding both thumbs up. What bad could happen to me today after that?

The Firm's Oakland office was originally a sub-office of the San Francisco office. It was started to serve Rineholt Corporation, a major client headquartered in Oakland. Quentin Barnes and a skeleton crew were sent over from San Francisco and in less than five years had built up a large enough core of clients in the East Bay to justify the office's autonomy. I joined The Firm right after Oakland became a separate office.

The office is located on the eighth floor of the Merritt Plaza Building. The offices on one side of the building look out over the Bay and San Francisco, and the offices on the other side look out over Lake Merritt and the Oakland hills, where I was raised and where Libby and I live. Both views are spectacular, and there are no bad offices, although I especially like mine because it looks out over the Bay.

Another advantage of our office is the parking. We have enough tenant-reserved spaces in the building so that everyone who is in the office can get a space. In public accounting, a large portion of the professional staff is at clients' offices during the work day. We have about fifty professionals on staff and thirty-five allocated parking spaces for "comers and goers." This works out fine as long as we schedule staff meetings after 5:00 P.M., when other tenants have gone home.

When I arrived at the office, I went through my normal routine for days when I go into the office instead of directly to a client. I said good morning to Janine, our receptionist; grabbed a cup of coffee from the staff room; said good morning to Marie, the secretary I share with the other audit managers; and went into my office, checked my voicemail for messages, and began to plot my strategy for the day. Of course, today would be different, and all I could actually do was think about my meeting with Barnes.

I had hoped that a message from Barnes's office would be waiting for me, but there wasn't one. I went out to check with Marie; she saw me coming and preempted me.

"There's no message from Mr. Barnes yet, Jack. Take it easy—no one has died from this yet."

"Thanks, Marie. You sound like you've been talking to Libby."

"We talk, Jack, but not about you," she grinned. Why did I have the feeling that Marie was really having fun with this?

Janine paged me just as I entered the staff room to get my second cup of coffee: *Jack Butler, please call extension 4002.* That was Madeline Stovall's number. Madeline is Quentin Barnes's executive assistant—actually, his keeper. Madeline is in her early fifties and looks like a model for *Vogue* magazine's matron section. She is always polite, gives people a wonderful smile, and then tells them exactly the way it is and forever will be. She runs interference for Barnes in a way no running back ever could. Madeline has been known to put in a good word with Barnes or do small favors for people she likes. She can also be intimidating, especially to newer staff members. Life in the office is easier for those who gain favor with Madeline Stovall, and I had always tried my best to do so.

As I approached Madeline's desk, she gave me her special smile, the one that comes with a little softening of her eyes. This is her loving, sincere smile, and it made me feel more at ease, even a little bit hopeful. "Go on in, Jack. Mr. Barnes is waiting for you." The moment had arrived.

The best way to describe Quentin Barnes is with his nickname, "The Bear"— or, more endearingly, just "Bear." Bear is large physically: 6'3" and well over 200 pounds. He was a swimmer in college and has those long legs and large chest and shoulders that swimmers develop. Over the years, Bear has filled out, and now he is considered overweight. In fact, his wife, Sally, and his friends worry that his weight could cause him health problems. But Bear enjoys a good meal as much as the next person, so his weight is a constant struggle.

Bear has dark brown hair and light brown eyes. He has thick hair on his arms and chest that sometimes protrudes above his collar. He does not have a particularly dark complexion, but he has a thick beard that provides a 5 o'clock shadow by 2:30 in the afternoon. The main thing about Bear is his general tenor and behavior. He leads with his eyes and follows with his body, and then his voice. He can smile or glare with those eyes in a way that lets people know exactly how he feels and how they should feel. (I often muse about who could outstare the other, Bear or Madeline.) And then he can well up and move his body forward in a way that can be welcoming or intimidating. Finally, the booming voice: It comes after one knows he has observed and thought—it can laugh, it can approve, or it can admonish. By the time the voice comes, there is no turning away. Bear definitely knows how to get your attention and to make his point.

I have a good relationship with The Bear, perhaps even more than good. We got off to a fine start during the recruiting process. I had gone to Farwestern State University, as he had, and we both share a great love for Farwestern State football. Bear hasn't missed an FSU football game since he was a freshman, and Libby and I go to several games a year with Quentin and Sally. Bear also likes to play golf, which is my specialty. I've played golf with him many times, and it is always fun for both of us. But I've often suspected that another reason Bear likes me and has allowed me to become his friend is that he and Sally don't have any children, and at times he may think of me as the son he never had.

When I walked into Bear's office, he was standing in front of his desk. He flashed a Madelinelike smile and extended his hand. "Congratulations, Jack! I've never been happier to tell someone they've been admitted to The Firm."

I must have looked like a light bulb that someone just turned on. I could feel my mouth widen and my face tighten. I realized that my imaginings of this moment didn't come close to how great it felt. My stomach stopped quivering and all the anxiety of the past few days disappeared. I could feel a rush of warmth throughout my body. But, as articulate as I wanted to be, my head was buzzing and I couldn't think of anything profound to say at the moment. I simply said, "Thanks, Bear. This means a lot to me. Believe me, The Firm will never be sorry it made this decision."

Bear knew what I was going through—he had been there himself. He put his arm around my shoulder and gave me a hug. He said, "You'll come down to earth in a few days, and then we can talk about what partnership really means. In the meantime, here's a letter addressed to you from Arnold Mackalry in the national office giving you all the administrative details of becoming a partner. You'll have to go to a meeting in New York in a couple of weeks to sign and seal things up. Arnold's office will make the travel arrangements. If you have any questions about this stuff, or any problems, just give Arnold a call."

"Sounds great, Bear."

"Jack, the reason I didn't call you in first is that I like to tackle the tough problems before the easy ones. I talked to Don and I'm afraid he didn't make it. He's very disappointed, as he should be. I know you and he are close friends. I expect he'll need some extra support right now."

When I heard this, my feelings began to sink. Don and I had gone to college together, and, next to Libby, he was my best friend. I guess I knew this was going to happen. I was afraid Don was going through the agony I had imagined during the night. The worst part was that because there was room for only one new audit partner, I felt that my success had at least partially been realized at the price of Don's failure.

"What are his options?" I asked.

"Well, he certainly doesn't have to leave The Firm. He does a great job solving technical problems. He could stay here as a manager, or he could transfer back to the national office and hope to become a technical reference partner. He's pretty good with clients, but he just hasn't been able to bring in any new business. You know, Jack, it's always a numbers game. If you want to be a partner, you have to have a client base, and if we increase the size of the partnership, there has to be an increase in our volume to support it."

"Yeah, well, I've got to be honest with you, Bear. I wish there were a way Don could be feeling as good as I do now. It just seems to me that a process like this shouldn't inflict so much pain on some while it gives pleasure to others."

"I know how you feel, Jack; I feel the same way. But the reality is that Don wouldn't have been promoted this year whether you were or not. You made it on your merits; Don didn't, based on his. And besides, two out of three isn't bad; Barbara got admitted too."

"Now that is good news. I'll have two things to celebrate tonight."

"Why don't you go and call Libby? Sally knows about this and she's delighted. I still have to talk to Barbara, so if you see her in the hall, keep a straight face. You can talk to Barbara after I do."

5

So I left Bear's office feeling great, but with just a little apprehension about poor Don. As I said, Don Parnell and I had gone to college together. We both went on to graduate school, although he got a master's in accountancy and I went into the one-year MBA program. We joined The Firm together, along with two others from Farwestern State: Norma Costansa, the president of Beta Alpha Psi, and Harry Blackmer, who went into tax. Norma and Harry left The Firm after they became CPAs; Don and I both stayed on. We both found that we liked the work we were doing, thought the Oakland office was a great place to work, and were satisfied that we were making good progress in terms of regular advancement and compensation.

Not only were Don and I close as colleagues and as friends, so were our wives, having been sorority sisters in college. Don and Dee Dee got married right after he graduated. They introduced Libby and me and went with us on our first date. Their daughter, Clair, is like a big sister to our kids. Now I was a partner and Don wasn't: How would that affect our relationship and Libby and Dee Dee's? What a mess.

When I got back to my office, I winked at Marie, who mouthed, "Congratulations," and then I went in and called Libby. There was no answer and my immediate thought was, How could Libby have the temerity to be gone at a time like this? I paused and laughed at myself. Of course she could be gone. The woman had a thousand things to do. All I could do was say, "Call me, I've got good news," to the answering machine.

I walked over to Don's office. He wasn't in. I asked Marie if she knew where he was, and she said he left after he met with Mr. Barnes, saying only that he wouldn't be available today and would be back tomorrow. This surprised me. I didn't think Don would do anything stupid, but I didn't think he'd just leave the office either. I guess I was really just disappointed that he wasn't there to congratulate me and absolve me of the feelings of guilt I was having.

At that point I figured I didn't have much to do except read the partnership materials Bear had given me. I dug into them and found out what the partnership agreement says, how the pension plan works, and how I could finance my partnership capital. It looked to me like a sophisticated approach to the old "golden chain." As a young partner I would get a goodly amount of earnings, but by the time I paid my capital, kicked into the pension plan, and bought a few new suits, a car, and a house commensurate with my new station in life, there wouldn't be a lot of cash left over. The effect of this, of course, would be to motivate me to work even harder to try to get ahead. What did I expect? Partners worked harder than staff, and there were certainly reasons why. Money and status had to be part of it. I hoped the major part included enjoyment and satisfaction.

After an hour of reading, I went over and stuck my head into Barb Gillespie's office. She was just getting off the phone with her husband, Rob. We congratulated each other and agreed we'd get together for lunch to plan how we would "really make something of this firm together." I went back to the partnership documents, and after a few minutes, the phone rang; it was Libby. "Hey, Mr. Partner, congratulations!"

"Congratulations to you too, *Mrs.* Partner. What do you think?"

"That's *Ms.* Partner, buster, and I think it's wonderful. Of course, I knew you would make it all along. No surprise to me, worry-wart. Oh, and Sally Barnes called. She invited us to their house for dinner on Saturday night with the Gillespies. I'll bet Barb's excited."

"She sure is, but I'm afraid Don didn't make it."

"I know, Dee Dee called me. She said Don came home and was pretty upset. After he calmed down, they decided to drive up to Sacramento to see his folks. Do you think he'll go in with his father?" (Don Parnell comes from a family of accountants. His dad and uncle are both CPAs and have a firm in Sacramento.)

"I don't know, Libby; it's certainly a possibility. I feel that I've got to talk to Don. I hope he doesn't just make a rash decision. There are still alternatives for him here at The Firm."

"Well, he'll be back tomorrow and Dee Dee says he plans to call you. You know, Jack, if it were you, you sure wouldn't be thinking about continuing your career with The Firm, would you?"

"I guess not. It's hard to spend your life living just outside of the country club fence. Anyway, I'm going to have lunch with Barb, make a couple of calls, and then come home early. Go down to Lester's and get some caviar and champagne and we'll celebrate."

"I'm already one step ahead of you, lover. I'll send the kids over to Gloria's and see you soon."

Discussion Questions

1–1 Can one have a "successful" career in public accounting without being a partner in a firm?

1–2 Is it possible—or desirable—to separate one's life as a professional from one's life as a person?

1–3 How important are personal relationships, with both management and support staff, in "getting ahead" in a public accounting firm, or any other business?

1–4 How does the personality of the partner in charge affect an accounting practice?

1–5 What is the nature of the "numbers problem" with becoming a partner in a public accounting firm? How are some firms dealing with this problem?

1–6 What are the financial aspects of partnership?

2
Celebration

Barbara Gillespie and I went to Franchot's for lunch. It's a quiet, semi-dark place that has private booths, the better to plot in. We actually didn't do much plotting. We ordered a drink—in violation of office policy, I might add—and sat back to participate in a kind of mutual gloating exercise.

Barbara Gillespie is a very impressive person. She has a joint business/tax degree from Belmont College, a private school down on the Peninsula. She graduated with honors and joined The Firm the year before I did. She's married to Rob Gillespie, a successful attorney in practice in San Francisco. She is a trim, attractive brunette who is feminine and all business. Whenever I have a tax question, I always go to Barbara for help, rather than to Roy Shantz—not only because I think she's the top tax person in the office, but also because she's so nice to work with.

Barbara likes me too. There are occasions when she needs to let off a little steam to someone in the office, and she invariably talks to me. She trusts me, and frankly, I'm glad she does talk to me. I sort of feel as if she's the older sister I never had, and I welcome the chance to give her support. I like Barbara's husband, Rob, too. Libby and I do things socially with Barb and Rob, and Rob and I play golf together when we get the chance.

After a while, although it was not my intention, our conversation took a turn. "You know, Jack, while I'm absolutely gratified by this promotion, I can't help but have some feelings of resentment at the same time."

"What do you mean, Barb?" My antennae went up.

"Well, compare the two of us. I have a law degree in addition to an MBA, and I have a year's more experience than you do. I'm twice as good as some of those clowns who got promoted to partner last year, but I was held back. You know why, don't you, Jack? Because I'm a woman."

"I know it's tougher for women in business than it is for men, Barb, but I thought public accounting was way ahead of other fields."

"It is, Jack, kicking and screaming. Over half of the accounting graduates these days are women. But only about 10 percent of our partners are women. I'll bet only 10 percent of our group this year will be women when the list comes out. I have to carry so much extra 'baggage' just to hold even that it tires me out some days. Look at your rise to glory here. You had Quentin mentoring you. I didn't have a mentor because there aren't any women partners in the office."

"Well, I can understand how you feel, Barb . . ."

"No, you can't," she interrupted.

"Okay, I'll *try* to understand how you feel, then. I was just going to say that I felt Quentin was behind you 100 percent, and that had he been the tax partner, he would have been a strong mentor for you."

"Yeah, you're right about Quentin, but for me, he's no substitute for a woman I could talk to. Oh, Jack, I'm sorry I'm blowing all this off on you. You're my best friend in the office and I just need to get this off my chest before I forget it and go on with a still more brilliant career."

"Hey, no problem. All I ask is that you let me ride along on your coat-tails."

"Be my guest. You know, the worst was when Stan Wright was here. I don't think I ever told you about this, but Stan's gone now and I suspect you'll appreciate hearing it because I know there was no love lost between you and Stan."

Stan Wright was a manager in the office who left a couple of years ago. In short, Stan was a jerk. He was awful to work for. He reminded me of what working a patch of land during the days of feudalism must have been like. He pushed the staff way too hard and had no sympathy for anyone's personal situation. I worked under Stan on an engagement a few years ago and it was a miserable experience, but I didn't realize Barbara had had any problems with him.

Barbara continued, "The first year I was a manager, I was assigned to review the tax accrual for Portland Iron. Stan was the audit manager, so I reported to him. I figured it was a two-day job. Anyway, after the first day, Stan gathered everybody in the little conference room we were using and went around the table asking everyone for a 'report' of what they had accomplished that day. After the staff summarized what they had done, Stan would 'quiz' them. Actually, what he did was badger and belittle them. He was the classic case of the authority figure who tries to make himself feel better by making others feel worse. I could hardly stand to sit there and watch what was going on.

"When Stan got to me, he introduced me as 'The Tax Queen' and asked if I liked 'coming down' to the field and 'gracing them' with my 'royal presence.' I gave him one of my best glares and said that I spent most of my time in the field this time of year and was happy to be able to see the individual staff members because they were out of the office so much. Then Stan sort of leered at me and said that in my honor, he wanted to end the day on a happy note, and asked—I guess I'd say, ordered—one of the staff to tell a joke. The poor staff guy just withered and mumbled that he didn't know any good jokes. Stan said he'd heard a good one, so he'd tell the joke. I won't re-peat the joke, Jack, even if I could remember it. It was gross, and the whole time Stan was telling it, he stared at me. I know he was trying to embarrass me. The staff was certainly embarrassed; they couldn't wait to get out of there.

"When Stan finished the joke, he laughed at it a lot harder than anyone else did. I just glared at him. I think he enjoyed that the most. Anyway, he sent the staff home and told me he wanted a word before I left. When we were alone, he asked me if I liked the joke. I said I had heard my share of off-color stories over the years and this one wouldn't rank as one of my favorites. I told him that I knew he was trying to embarrass me in front of the staff and that I had heard he was a jerk and now I knew it for a fact.

"Then he gave me his biggest leer and said, 'I'm not a jerk, Barbara, I'm really a nice guy. You're going to have to put up with a lot of crap from men if you want to get ahead in business, and I just want to help you out with a little on-the-job training. If the joke bothered you because you don't like sex, I can understand that. But you impress me as the kind of girl who can hold her own in that department.'"

"You're kidding," I said. I always thought Stan was the worst, but this was a totally new side of him I hadn't considered. "What did you do?"

"I stood up, grabbed my coat and briefcase, and walked to the door. When I got there, I turned around and, in my best Bette Davis fashion, I told him, 'Stan, I am putting you on official notice that you have offended me and I consider your actions to be sexual harassment. I am an attorney as well as a CPA. I plan to document this incident thoroughly. When I arrive here tomorrow morning, I expect a sealed note on my desk containing your formal apology. If I don't get it, or if you *ever* step out of line with me or any other woman in the office like this again, I'm going to nail you to the wall. Have you got that, Stan?'

"He hemmed and hawed and said he didn't mean anything by it, that he was only trying to be friendly, that he was only kidding. But next morning, the apology was there, and he stayed as far away from me as he could for the rest of the time he was with the firm."

"Jeez, that's great, Barb. I wish I could have been there. What did Rob say?"

"I didn't tell him until months after it happened. I figured this was the kind of thing I had to deal with on my own. I can't expect to run home to Rob every time something difficult happens to me at work. Would you have gone to Libby if some female on the staff had come on to you?"

"No, I guess not."

"Jack, you're the only other person I've told about this. I confided in you because I know you're someone I can trust."

"Message received, Barb. You don't have to worry about me." Barb gave me a smile and reached over and squeezed my hand. "Watch it," I joked. We both laughed and ate our lunches in the same good mood we'd had when we came in. We mused about becoming the partners in charge of the audit and tax departments some day, perhaps even partner in charge of the office. I told Barbara that if either of us would be PIC, it should be she— I never could have handled Stan the way she did.

After Barbara Gillespie and I got back to the office, I returned a couple of calls, thanked a few people who came in to congratulate me (the grapevine was fast at work), and headed down to Moran's Jewelers on the arcade floor of our building. I knew that Libby deserved just as much credit for my success as I did, and I wanted to get something for her to express my thanks. I selected a sterling silver pendant that had a large, scripted "L" on it. It was tasteful and not too lavish. Libby is the family budget officer, so I didn't want to offend her financial sensibilities. I wanted to get something that was just right. I also went to the florist for roses and to See's for chocolates. I know all the woman's weaknesses.

When I got home, Libby was waiting for me. She had the kids dressed up and they had made a card for me with crayons and poster paper. They drew a picture of me and "wrote," with Mom's help, "Congratulations, Dad. You are the best Dad in the world, and we love you." It was enough to make me start tearing up. I gave the kids a hug and a kiss. Libby gave me a hug and went to put the roses in water. When she got back, she gave each of the kids their choice of a chocolate and told them to say goodbye to Daddy because she was going to take them over to Aunt Gloria's house to spend the night. That was fine with them; Gloria and Al loved the kids as much as we did, and they would all be in for a big evening.

Libby had gone to the market with a vengeance. She got rib steaks, mushrooms, potatoes and onions, Caesar salad makings, and cherry ice cream for dessert—all of my favorite things. She had gotten a bottle of champagne and put it on ice. I barbecued the steaks while she put the rest together, and then we went to the table to eat. It was too early for candlelight, but Libby set the mood by putting her arms around my neck and giving me a serious kiss. "My hero." She said this laughingly, but I secretly hoped she really meant it.

"Oh, Lib. We've worked damned hard for this—let's enjoy the moment. I'm only thirty-two, I've got a lot of years still ahead of me, and it isn't really going to get any easier, but the lid's off now. There's no reason why we can't do as well as we want."

Libby said that she knew partners worked harder than anybody, and she was prepared for it. The main things she wanted were stability at home, as many complete weekends as we could have together, and the ability to plan and take great vacations while the kids were at home. I wanted these things too, and I was worried that partnership could put a strain on our family. There were horror stories in The Firm about partners' never taking vacations or being called back in the middle of them. There was also a fairly high divorce rate among partners. I felt confident of Libby's support, but I also knew that evenings and weekends alone with the children would be wearing at best. I vowed to keep things in balance for all of us.

After dinner we sat and talked some more and did the dishes together. For a moment, I started to turn on the TV to see how the Giants were doing, but I caught myself. Instead, I suggested we go to the bedroom, turn on some good music, and finish off the champagne. Libby thought that was a good idea too. Romance was in the air at the Butler castle.

Later in the evening, Libby was asleep and I was still wired. I lay in bed going over the events of an incredible day. I was content. I had a great family, good friends (I vowed that my friendship with Don would be even stronger), and now I was a *partner*, with all the perks and prestige that went with the position. For me, that meant belonging to a private golf club, one of my life's great goals. I was a six handicap when I got out of college and had ballooned to a twelve. Now scratch was in sight.

Finally, I started to think about all the things that had happened to me—college, choosing The Firm to go to work for, my first training program, clients I had worked with, and my experiences with various partners and staff. I felt as if I had my life as under control as possible. I had only two worries—how to help Don, and how to make sure I didn't step in front of a moving vehicle and get killed before I signed the partnership agreement. Oh well, I would see Don tomorrow and things would take care of themselves. I finally drifted off to sleep, a different person from the one I was when I'd gotten up that morning.

Discussion Questions

2–1 Is there a "glass ceiling" in public accounting, and what special problems do women in the profession face?

2–2 What is the nature, both legally and socially, of sexual harassment? Is it more or less prevalent in public accounting than in other areas of business?

2–3 What are some of the strains that a career in public accounting can place on one's personal and family life? Is this any different from the way it is in other careers? How important is support from one's spouse and/or others in these situations?

3

School Days

When I was a junior in high school, I was the number-one player on the Mountainside golf team by three strokes. I was playing state junior tournaments and doing very well. I could see graduating from high school as a named player and getting scholarship offers from all the big golf schools. That was my dream; unfortunately, it evaporated when I was injured in an automobile accident early in my senior year. I had to have surgery on my left leg, leaving it a little shorter than my right. I acquired a scar and a limp and lost my future as a big-time golfer. I've struggled to get my game back ever since, but I can't complain; I'm alive, and if I can't become the world's greatest golfer, I can sure as hell be a great accountant.

I didn't start out intending to study accounting. I wanted to be a lawyer, like my dad. My father, Art Butler, is a partner in Messner, Smith and Bolter in San Francisco. He specializes in corporate law and has always made the law sound incredibly interesting. Dad would tell stories at dinner at night about his experiences during the day. He'd emphasize the human aspects behind his clients' legal problems and he'd do it with sarcasm and humor; he would always have us laughing. Dad could do legal standup.

My mom, Susan Butler, like Libby, has always been the stabilizer of the family. Like most mothers during the first decades after World War II, she was a homemaker. Mom studied English/Lit in college and loves to read. She writes occasional columns for the Montclair weekly newspaper, teaches reading at the Oakland Library, and does other volunteer work.

I also have two sisters, Eileen and Jennifer. Eileen is married and lives in Chicago with her husband, Ralph, who is with IBM. Jennifer teaches high school English in San Luis Obispo, having followed somewhat in Mom's footsteps. We named our Jenny after her.

Since I couldn't go to a big golf school as planned, Farwestern State University looked like the best place for me to go to college. It had a great law school and a good business program, which Dad had advised me was the best course of pre-law study for corporate law. Plus, FSU was close to home. I could live at home and enjoy Mom's cooking, or, if I felt the need, I could live near school and still enjoy her cooking. This seemed like the best of all worlds. Finally, Abbey Fuhriman was planning to go to FSU. Abbey was a cheerleader at Mountainside and although she wasn't one of my active girl-friends, I figured if we went to college together, things might move in that direction. As it turned out, that event didn't materialize.

I had done pretty well in high school, making the top third of my class. I did very well on my SATs and got accepted at FSU. I found college inter-esting enough, but I always found other things I really liked to do, specifi-cally skiing and golf. I know that sounds strange in light of my leg injury, but what better way was there to overcome the accident than to build up the leg with exercises for strength and coordination? I was off to the slopes every chance I got in the winter, and off to the links every chance I got during the spring, summer, and fall. In addition, I always had some kind of a part-time job. Although my folks were contributing a significant amount of money toward my college education, I always needed something extra.

The bottom line of the Jack Butler college lifestyle was that in my freshman year, my grades weren't as good as they should have been. This frustrated my father because he was concerned that I might not get into a top-level law school or develop the kind of study habits I would need to get me through law school at a high enough level to make me attractive to the better law firms. My attitude was that I was doing fine and that he shouldn't worry. It was only my first year, and I had everything under control. I could "turn it on" anytime I wanted to. Dad said that this attitude was denial and self-delusion and that my grades were in the record and would come back to haunt me. He said that at least 80 percent of the admissions criteria at most law schools were based on GPA and the LSAT, and that, whereas I was strong on personal attributes, I had to give my grades a higher priority.

In my sophomore year I experienced an academic epiphany: I took my first accounting course and I got my first A. Not only that, I really liked the course. My instructor was an interesting guy, an adjunct professor who had an active accounting practice. He talked to us about business situations and how good information was a key to business success. He not only helped his clients with their taxes and accounting systems, he also gave the principals personal financial advice. He seemed to be a sort of financial "doctor," ready to solve all kinds of problems. He said that because of the importance of in-formation, accountants were instrumental to any business. When I took my second accounting course and got another A, I decided to narrow my pre-law study to getting an accounting degree. Dad thought that was great—anything to get me engrossed enough to push my grade point average toward the skies.

Majoring in accounting turned out to be a sound decision. FSU had (and still has) a great accounting faculty and, I've since found out, pays much more attention to individual student needs than do most large univer-sities. When I became a junior, I was officially admitted to the accounting program. I was put with a cohort of students who would go through the ac-counting series together. More important, I was assigned to a faculty mem-ber who would be my counselor for the next two years. My counselor was

Wally Garner, a wonderful teacher and a great friend. Wally was responsible for looking after about twenty students split between their junior and senior years. He maintained constant contact with each of us individually, but he also liked to get us together as a group. He referred to us as "Wally's Raiders."

Wally's Raiders all became good friends. In my junior year, it was very helpful to have contact with the seniors, who had all kinds of good advice about such things as getting through tough courses, deciding whether to go to graduate school, and surviving the recruiting process. And when I was a senior, I found I was looking after some of the new juniors. I came to realize that Wally was teaching us how to develop relationships and mentoring skills. We were also competitive. In one sense, this caused us to work against one another to some extent, but the conventional wisdom was that the business world was competitive, and we needed to be prepared for it as realistically as possible. One member of our group had T-shirts made up with "Wally's Raiders" on them. We had softball and volleyball teams that entered intramural competition. We had a Friday night drinking club and all met at Moon's Bar after school for camaraderie and fun. Wally and his wife, Rosy, attended whenever they could. I look back on those days as some of the best times of my life.

Wally taught management accounting in FSU's MBA program and auditing in both the undergraduate and graduate programs. He was a CPA and had worked for one of the large firms before going back to Illinois to get his doctorate. He did most of his research in auditing and was particularly interested in how auditors made the judgments they made.

The first time I met with Wally, we talked about whether I should take a minor or not. This was an option at FSU. I could graduate without one; but with a little extra coursework, I could have a minor specified on my diploma. Wally talked about a number of possibilities and then asked me which courses outside of accounting I had taken and really liked. My response was statistics. This surprised Wally because most students seemed to shy away from statistics. Wally said that statistics would be a wonderful minor for an accounting student, because there are so many ways statistics can be used in accounting and business in general. When I told him that I planned to become a lawyer, not an accountant, Wally said that was okay, and that I should still minor in statistics. He also added that he hoped I would not mind if, as time went on, he tried to change my view of a career in accounting. Wally had me charmed by that time—of course I didn't mind his attempts.

The longer I studied accounting, the more I liked it. The accounting program had regular speakers from the accounting profession, both public and industry, and I liked what I heard. The profession was dynamic and in a period of rapid growth. Accountants were thought of as professionals and given a great deal of latitude in how they did things. And there was a lot to the work in terms of both challenge and variety. Finally, it sounded as if the potential for advancement and significant income was very good.

Slowly but surely, I started thinking about going into accounting rather than into law. By the middle of my senior year, I had just about made the decision to change my path. Of course, the big problem was that I didn't want to disappoint Dad. Over Christmas vacation the subject came up. Dad pointed out that law school applications had to be in at most schools by the middle of February.

"Dad, I've been meaning to get your advice about that. The fact is, I've been thinking about maybe going into accounting instead of law."

"Oh, really. That's interesting. Why do you think you should do that?"

"Well, I really like accounting and I'm doing great in all my classes. I've heard speakers from the accounting profession, and there's tremendous opportunity there. And, to be honest with you, Dad, I think law is your thing, not mine."

Dad looked at me and I felt awful. I didn't want to disappoint him, but he had always told me to be honest and open with him. When I was eleven he was my Little League coach and it seemed as if he were getting on me more than the other kids. I know he wanted me to be a great ball player. After one incident where I dropped a fly ball, I started to cry. When Dad saw that, he realized that he had been pressuring me. He told me that he was sorry, that he loved me, and that I should always tell him when something he did seemed wrong or unfair to me, that he'd understand.

After a thoughtful pause, Dad stood me up and put his hands on my shoulders. "I think you'll make a great accountant, Jack. Heck, there are too many lawyers anyway, and I can tell you there's plenty of need for more good accountants. I'm glad you've made up your own mind about what you want to do, and you sure have my blessing."

I was so relieved, and I felt as if the light of day had just begun to shine on me. I gave my excuses and left to go to a movie with one of my friends. But as I left, I saw Mom mouth, "Way to go, Art" and give Dad a smile. Watch out, accounting profession—here I come! I had not only chosen the field I thought was for me, but it had been my decision, and my decision alone.

During my senior year, I got to know Wally pretty well. I got a part-time job grading papers for his basic auditing course, a course that I had taken the previous year. He and I started to have conversations about my career. As we discussed my options, I discovered that most of them involved graduate school. Wally convinced me that whatever aspect of accounting I pursued, investing in another year of study would provide a significant payback, in terms of both opportunities and earnings potential. And he pointed out that it was only a matter of time before all states would require 150 hours of formal education in order for someone to become a CPA. At the time I graduated, more and more students were getting graduate degrees, and those without them were becoming disadvantaged.

FSU had both a master's of professional accountancy (MPrA) program and a masters of business administration (MBA) program. The MPrA program, which lasted nine months, was terrific for people who wanted to specialize in systems or tax. All the tax graduates got snapped up by the CPA firms. The MBA program could be completed in twelve months with a bachelor's degree in business. The MBA program also provided for an emphasis in accounting where courses in the MPrA program were taken as electives.

The first career option I considered was to go into industry. About 40 percent of our graduates followed that path. I had met a number of my father's friends who worked in financial positions with corporations that his firm served, and most of them seemed prosperous and very interested in what they were doing. Wally made the argument that as an officer of a corporation, one could be granted stock options, which was the way many businesspeople acquired their fortunes. Of course, it was unlikely that I could move from graduation directly into being a CFO. There would be many years of hard work in between, and getting into the corporate pipeline seemed risky to me. If a person went with an overly stable company, he or she could go for years without any movement. I knew that most people in my situation would change jobs four or five times during their careers. On the other hand, a lot of people who went with high-tech growth companies made their way in no time. Nevertheless, I was somewhat ambivalent about starting down that path. I guess I wanted a situation with more control over my career than industry seemed to provide.

The second option was to go to work for government. Both state and federal agencies offered a variety of interesting positions. The Chief Accountant for the Securities and Exchange Commission had been a speaker at FSU. The guy was an excellent speaker and clearly had led a rewarding professional life. He had dealt with major accounting and reporting problems involving the biggest and most important companies. His judgments influenced accounting decisions throughout the country. I knew people who had gone with the state Auditor's Office, which was actually like a big CPA firm. I also knew a woman who went with the FBI. Government was not the highest-paying option, but it was certainly worth considering; it offered interesting and challenging career opportunities and could provide a great deal of satisfaction from knowing that one's efforts contributed to the common good.

My third option was to become an internal auditor. Many large companies in the Bay Area have internal audit staffs. Wally pointed out that an internal auditor learned absolutely everything there was to know about a company, and for that reason, internal audit was often a training ground for entry into operations and higher-level management. Internal auditors generally have to travel a lot, but for some people, that is an enticement.

My final two options were both in public accounting: to become a CPA in one of the large firms or in a regional or local firm. I had talked to my dad about all of my career options, and he persuasively argued that I should become a CPA. He felt that with a CPA certificate I would always have options with my career. Like a lawyer, I could "hang out my shingle" and make a good living doing tax returns, small audits, small-business consulting, and personal financial planning—services generally provided by sole practitioners. Wally made a stronger argument. He said that many successful accounting and financial executives started out with CPA firms, received excellent exposure to a number of businesses and training, and then jumped into industry. He said that after a number of years in public accounting, the transition was often to a position that was higher than would be attained by going directly into industry.

The more I thought about it and consulted with Wally and my father, the more comfortable I felt with the decision to become a CPA. My strategy was to go to work for one of the large firms, primarily because they had most of the publicly held companies as their clients. I felt that experience with companies dealing with the SEC would better serve me as a potential CFO. I would learn big-company skills and make contacts in companies for which I might want to work. But I would also interview with regional and local firms. I couldn't see the downside in not interviewing with as many firms as I could manage. The market was pretty good in the previous year, so I was confident I would get a position with a CPA firm. After a few years developing myself, I'd move over into industry—as a CFO, I hoped. I'm not sure why, but the thought of staying with the firm I went to work for and becoming a partner didn't stand very high on my list of possibilities or goals at that point in time. I had heard that the great majority of people who entered public accounting left prior to partnership, so it may be that I just didn't think that my becoming a partner was very realistic.

My two best friends in my cohort, Don Parnell and Arch Melvin, made somewhat different decisions from mine. Don's father and uncle were owners of a local CPA firm in Sacramento. Don's plan was to get his MPrA, go to work for a larger firm in the Bay Area, and then go with his father and uncle after he had honed his technical skills. Parnell & Parnell wasn't doing a lot of audits, so Don thought he could give them the ability to extend their practice. Arch, on the other hand, decided to forgo getting a graduate degree and to go directly with the local firm he had been working part-time for during undergraduate school. Arch made a very strong case for working for a local firm. He said that everyone was close—it was like a family. Even as a part-timer, he was involved in everything that went on. He got to know the clients well and would work with the owners of his clients' companies, not just the subordinates. He was given a great deal of responsibility even as a new staff member. Finally, Arch was very excited about his firm's growing service base in the litigation support field, doing investigative work and analyses to support lawyers actively involved in litigation. Arch had worked on a couple of these engagements and found them fascinating. He even looked forward to the possibility of testifying as an expert witness someday.

As to whether I should get an MPrA or an MBA degree, I decided to get the MBA. One reason was that I thought it would give me a better background for an eventual position in industry. However, Wally also suggested another good reason: that public accounting practice was essentially a broad communication process. CPAs communicate with clients about what they need them to do, they communicate with clients and with staff in doing it, and they communicate with clients and others about the results of their work once it is done. Everything involves communication, both oral and written. The big difference between the MPrA and MBA programs was that the MBA program focused more on communication and other behavioral skills. Wally said I could always learn more technology, but going into practice with strong communication skills was a major plus.

Of course, getting an MBA instead of an MPrA implied that I didn't want to become a systems consultant or a tax advisor. Through my decision, I was probably opting to become an auditor. When I talked to Wally about this aspect, he agreed that taxation was probably not in the cards. Consulting was always a possibility depending on the things I picked up as I gained experience doing audit engagements. With my statistics minor, I was a natural for some types of consulting engagements. But Wally, being an auditor by training and at heart, sold me on the idea that auditing offered a lot of advantages in terms of my professional development, and that I'd like it anyway.

Discussion Questions

3–1   What are the attractive/unattractive features of a career in accounting, in terms of each of the following?

   a. industry

   b. government

   c. internal audit

   d. public accounting—international and national

   e. public accounting—regional and local

3–2   What other career options might an accounting graduate have?

3–3   What are the advantages of going to graduate school, and within graduate school, the relative advantages of getting an MPrA or an MBA?

3–4   In a career in public accounting, what are the attractive/unattractive aspects of audit, tax, and management consulting as career paths?

4
Get a Job!

Graduate school turned out to be a very worthwhile experience, both in terms of learning more and developing my personal skills. The MBA program at FSU emphasized group work and the case method. I liked cases and I liked working with others. I found that I had a knack for organizing group work and for persuading the group when it needed persuading. We started in June, right after graduation, and spent the summer taking a six-credit course covering leadership, communications, and team building, as well as some technical update courses in accounting, finance, and marketing. The purpose of the technical courses was to emphasize the importance of actually remembering the stuff we study and to be able to use it in the future—something we didn't do very well as undergraduates. It also got us going on the case method.

Our more conventional courses began in the fall. That was the same time that recruiting by the accounting firms started. The kickoff event was called "Meet the Firms Night," where representatives from the accounting firms set up booths in a big auditorium-type room. Undergraduate and graduate students interested in public accounting could walk around, talk to the reps, and get their recruiting literature. The main idea for those who would interview was to make a good first impression so that firms would include them in their interview schedules. Generally, each firm would interview between 13 and 52 students in a season (one interviewer could conduct 13 interviews in a day). So with 160 accounting students looking for a job, competition for interview slots was fierce.

After meeting some of the firms' representatives, I went home and looked at their recruiting brochures. I was reminded of an old story about San Francisco's Chinese restaurants—that there was only one giant kitchen underground in Chinatown that did all the cooking for all the restaurants. The brochures looked almost the same, as if they had been written by one source and then packaged a little differently from the others. I was caught by the number of brochures that concluded with a picture of a handsome young couple with one or two handsome young children on a picnic, enjoying life in public accounting!

Following my plan, I signed up for ten interviews. I had no idea how hectic things would be, trying to balance all of the things I had to worry about at that particular time. But I figured it was worth the effort. The routine for the interviews was pretty standard. I would go to the Placement Center prior to the interview time. A staff person who had been well known at FSU and had gone to work for the interviewing firm would be there to greet me and warm me up. I called these the "Ed McMahon people." Then I would go in and spend thirty minutes with the interviewer. The interviewer would probably be a manager, but maybe a partner. In the year I interviewed it was always a man; I know that that has changed in the last few years. In a couple of cases, the interviewer was a full-time human resources person, and one of these was a regional interviewer who was hiring for offices all over the west coast.

The purpose of the interview, of course, was to get some impression of me beyond what my transcript, reference letters, and resumé showed. I'm sure the interviewer also wanted to make a good impression on me and convince me that his firm was the best one for which to work.

The conventional wisdom, communicated to us by the Placement Office, was that the firms were interested in candidates who had good grades, significant work experience, rich living experiences (whatever that meant), extracurricular activities, organizational skills, interpersonal and communication skills, technical skills, ability to accept responsibility and learn on the job, a strong sense of commitment, and, they hoped, a facility with a second language. We all joked that there was only one valid candidate and he went into carpentry 2,000 years ago.

The interview questions ran in pretty much the same pattern irrespective of firm. They started out with a warm-up question like: What did I think of the FSU basketball team's chances of making the NCAA tournament this year? And, What courses did I enjoy most? The interview then moved on to more insightful "tell me" questions, such as: Tell me about a big project you had to plan for school or work. Describe a situation when you had several things to do in a limited time and how you handled it. Tell me about a time you helped resolve a group problem. After the first two interviews, I was well prepared to answer those questions. Then, during the last five to ten minutes, there came the time for me to ask any questions I might have about the interviewer's firm or about public accounting in general. The farewell was always, "It was great to meet you, Jack. If you have any questions at all that I didn't answer, please call me at any time."

The outcome of the interview would be a follow-up call and/or letter that would either tell me in a nice way that I was no longer on the firm's candidate list or invite me in for an office interview. I made a point of writing a thank-you letter to each interviewer the day of the interview. I wanted to make the best impression I could. I was hoping for enough office visits to provide good odds of obtaining at least one actual job offer.

My interview with The Firm started out about the same as the others when Andy Mickkelsen met me in the Placement Center. Andy said he loved working for The Firm—it was an exciting and energetic place to be. He felt that he was learning a great deal and getting more responsibility by the day. Then he said, "You're going to be talking with Quentin Barnes. He's the partner in charge of our Oakland office." I started to ask Andy about that when the receptionist said that I could go right in to Room E.

Interview Room E was set up with two chairs on either side of a small, round table. When I entered the room, Barnes was sitting on the far chair, shuffling through some papers he had in front of him. He jumped up and greeted me in his usual order of expression: a straight but smiling gaze, a big smile, and a booming, "Hi, Jack, how are you?"

"I'm fine," I replied. "How are you?"

"Great. I was wondering if you could help me with a problem I'm having. I'd appreciate your advice."

"Sure," I replied, totally puzzled about what he could possibly need my advice on.

"I understand that you got a minor in statistics in undergraduate school."

"That's right."

"Well, I've got two staff members who are having a little debate on one of my audits about whether they need to look at all of the contracts our client has in process or whether they can just do a sample. Normally, we sample all kinds of things, but in this case, there are only eight contracts. It takes about four hours of work for each contract, so if we sampled six of the contracts, we'd save a whole man-day of time. My senior wants to do the sample and my manager wants to do all eight. What do you think?"

What did I think? I thought, *This is worse than the SATs!* "Mr. Barnes, please don't be offended, but is this a real question, or is it some kind of an interview test?"

Barnes's response was an infectious laugh. "I swear, Jack, this is the real thing. I read your folder last night and I figured this was a chance for me to get some free advice."

"Okay. Well, if you're going to look at all but two of the contracts, and you assume that only one of them is wrong and seven are correct, I can tell you the odds of taking a random sample and getting all six correct. That would be 7 over 8 times 6 over 7 times 5 over 6 times 4 over 5 times 3 over 4 times 2 over 3. Let me show you." I wrote the fractions on a piece of paper and canceled the 3, 4, 5, 6, and 7 in both the numerator and denominator. "That leaves 1 over 4, or 25 percent. In other words, if one of the eight contracts were wrong, there would be a 75 percent chance, with a sample of six, that you would have selected it. If two of the contracts were wrong, the chances that you'd select one are much higher." I did a little more pencil pushing. "About 97 percent."

"That's terrific. So you think the sampling idea is all right, then?"

"I guess that would depend on whether you can live with one incorrect contract or two, and on what odds you think are acceptable. My impression from Wally Garner is that there are always circumstantial things to consider. Wally's stock answer is always 'It depends.'"

"Wally knows." Barnes then furrowed his brow and said, "Now, I actually have two problems. Let me ask you about the second one."

"All right."

"I've been having a terrible time with duck-hooking my drives lately. I've been told that you're a heck of a golfer, and you even give lessons to some of your friends. Can you help me out?"

Before I could answer, Barnes laughed and said, "Just kidding, Jack, but I would like to play golf with you some time."

By that time we were both in a pretty good mood, but then Barnes did turn a little more serious. "Let's talk about public accounting for a minute, Jack. Have you ever read *Walden*, by Henry David Thoreau?"

Walden? Thoreau? He wasn't an accountant. What was Barnes getting at now? "Yes, I have read it, but I think it was in high school, not in college. I can tell you it's one of my mother's favorite books."

"Thoreau said some things that have really stuck with me over the years. A lot of people think he was anti-business, but that's not true. Fundamentally, he was anti-*meaninglessness*. He didn't want to see his fellow beings spending their lives on meaningless activities and endeavors, working just to survive rather than spending their time doing things that are really gratifying to them.

"Jack, I want to make sure you understand what a career in public accounting would be like in those terms. First of all, public accounting can be a very meaningful profession. We do a great amount of good for a lot of people. We help our clients run their businesses better by giving them good tax and consulting advice, and we protect the people who invest billions of dollars each year through the capital markets by the audits we perform.

"The second thing is that most of us in public accounting really like what we do. It's interesting, there's tremendous variety to it, and there are lots of challenges. There's always a new situation to learn and a new set of problems to solve. You never know what's going to be on your desk when you come in in the morning, and you never know what surprises your next phone call will bring. And it pays well and offers a good career path, whatever a person's ultimate direction may be."

"Yes, I've thought about those things, although not in terms of *Walden*. I'm pretty convinced it's the right way for me to go."

"Good. Did Andy tell you that I was the partner in charge of our Oakland office?"

"Yes, he did."

"Have you wondered why I would take the time to come over here for these interviews? Believe me, I have plenty of other things to do."

"I guess I haven't."

"Well, I'll tell you. It's because my success and the success of The Firm rest almost entirely on how good a job we do in recruiting. Good people will lead us and poor people will kill us. It's that simple. I want you to know that. Another reason is that I have the authority to move ahead with office visits without making you dangle for a week. Can you come in next Friday?"

I couldn't believe it. "Yes, sure. Where do I go and at what time?"

"My assistant's name is Madeline Stovall. Madeline will call you at home tonight at six to give you the details, if that's all right."

Barnes stood up and extended his hand. "I've really enjoyed talking with you, Jack. Thanks for the statistical advice. I'll talk with you again next Friday. Also, be sure to give my regards to your father."

I was really caught off guard by this. "You know my father?"

"Oh, I thought you knew. He and I have a mutual client, First Women's Bank of the East Bay. He's the person who bragged to me about your golf game." The interview was over.

I had office visits with The Firm and two other large firms. I found them much less intimidating than the on-campus interviews. They were set up to make sure I felt at ease, got an idea of what the office was like, and became "friends" with everyone I met. The best part was lunch. At two of the firms, instead of going out with partners and managers, I was taken to a restaurant by three or four newer staff members. The purpose was to let me ask any and all questions I wouldn't feel comfortable asking a partner—to find out what things were *really* like in the office.

I received offers from The Firm and from one of the others. The other firm's offer was $800 per year more than The Firm's offer. I didn't feel that either offer was "negotiable." Both firms looked very attractive. It was time for another talk with Wally.

Wally seemed to know a great deal about both firms. He was also aware of the offers I had received. It became clear to me that the accounting firms must have a great deal of contact with the faculty during the recruiting process. Wally told me that before and during the time they were at school interviewing, the firms went over the names of the students with faculty and got their opinions about them. This was news to me, and I wished that I had known it beforehand. I somehow had assumed that my relationships with faculty were like my relationship with my doctor, based on a principle of confidence. When I expressed this to Wally, he saw my concern and assured me that he always made a practice of emphasizing the positive in these conversations. Nonetheless, I still felt uncomfortable.

When I asked Wally about the best way to decide between two firms, he said that he thought the large firms, as a whole, offered equal resources and opportunity, and that the main differences were at the local-office level. His advice was to choose on the basis of which firm I personally felt more comfortable with—where I felt I fit in best. His reason was that my long-term success would be the result of how good a job I did and that I would be more likely to do a good job in an environment in which I felt the most comfortable and had the fewest distractions.

My dad agreed with Wally, but he added another element. He believed, based on his law firm experience, that being assigned to the right clients and partners had a lot to do with how well one did. He said that firms logically put their best people on their most important clients. This created a halo effect; if you were assigned to an important client, the implication was that you must be a comer.

In the final analysis, I couldn't be sure which clients I would be assigned to, but I felt I would do a good job and prove myself in any case. I clearly felt more comfortable at The Firm, especially because of Quentin Barnes. I accepted The Firm's offer and spent the remaining seven months of graduate school enjoying the whole experience.

About midway through my MBA program, Wally asked to see me about "one additional thing." When we met in his office, he asked, "Have you got your network together yet?"

"What do you mean, Wally?" I asked.

"I know you don't plan to become a partner, Jack, but what if you find you really like public accounting and decide to stay? You have to realize that you can go only so far on job skills. If you want to make a career of it, you have to become a good business developer too. My suggestion is that you begin now to start a network of people you've met in college and with whom you'll deliberately keep in touch. You can add to it as time goes by. A lot of the people in your network will undoubtedly become as successful as you, and by the time you need to start promoting your firm, you'll have all these friends and contacts to work through to help you develop some business."

I thought about that for a moment and thanked Wally for sound advice well taken. I've often looked back on my time in school and realized that the mentoring program and my friendship with Wally were probably the two most important things FSU gave me.

Discussion Questions

4–1 What "soft" skills must you develop in school, and how might each be useful in public accounting?

4–2 How does the recruiting process work, what are recruiters looking for, and how should students prepare for and handle themselves during interviews?

4–3 What criteria should students use in deciding what company or firm to go to work for?

4–4 Why is formal networking important, and how can it be initiated and maintained?

5
Getting Started

The new class of junior staff members started in the Oakland office of The Firm on the same day—July 1. The office's client load wasn't as concentrated around calendar-year clients as in some offices and firms. There were a number of agricultural and governmental clients that had June 30 fiscal-year ends. And the office tried to concentrate interim work on Rineholt Corporation, its largest client, in July and August as much as possible. This meant that even though we would have some period of orientation, we would begin actual client work fairly quickly. This was a big relief to me, as I had heard horror stories of new staff spending large periods of time during their first two or three months sitting in the staff room with essentially nothing to do.

There were seven of us in our group: me, Don Parnell, Norma Costansa, and Harry Blackmer from FSU, Sid Renberg and Millie Truett from Cal State, and Cal Bennett from Carnegie-Mellon. Cal had been raised in Berkeley and gone away to college, always planning to return. He had written The Bear and gotten an interview and a job. All of us were going into audit, except Harry, who was in tax. Cal and I had MBAs; Norma, Don, and Harry had MPrAs; and Sid and Millie had BS degrees. Looking back, I'd say we were a pretty typical group, except that nowadays, one or two more of us would be women.

We met in the office's conference room for a greeting by The Bear. This is when we were introduced to Bearisms. He began, "Perhaps the most important thing for you all to know is that our clients are really two clients. There's the company that hires us, and there's the public that relies on the integrity of our work. Even though the largest group relying on our work is made up of investors and creditors, the government, the employees and their unions, and the communities our clients operate in rely on us as well. And our clients not only rely on us to do good audits, they also expect us to give them good tax advice and good business counsel as well. [Bearism No. 1.] So that means that while you're working for this or any other firm, you must carry a higher level of responsibility than just fulfilling a contract with a client to make a buck. You're here for the broader benefit of society as well.

Any time you see a conflict there, come and talk to me, and I guarantee you, I'll come down on the side of society. Of course, if you think about it, that's not only the right thing to do, it's also to our long-term benefit, isn't it?

"The Firm is a big firm, one of the biggest. As you'll find out soon enough, that means that by its nature, it's bureaucratic. We try to minimize the bureaucracy, but it can't be helped. The only way we can manage thousands of professionals and administrative staff is with some degree of bureaucracy. But I have learned one thing: Good audits are done by good auditors, good tax work is done by good tax professionals, and good consulting is done by good consultants. [Bearism No. 2.] All the policies and procedures, forms and manuals, and computer programs in the world won't make a poor professional into a good one. Only you can make yourself into a good professional. That's why I and the others in this office worked so hard to recruit you. That's why each of you is so important to us."

Bear had us by the eyes, ears, and minds by now, and he wasn't about to let go. "But this means that each of you is now faced with a set of major challenges. To start with, you have to do a good job—actually, better than just a good job. How are you going to do that? I have several suggestions for you. First, focus your attention on what you are doing at each moment and do it as well as you can. [Bearism No. 3.] If you show us that you can do a specific task well, we'll assume that you'll do any other task we ask of you well too. That's the way you get ahead in this firm, by doing one thing well at a time.

"Second, don't procrastinate; tackle the tough problems first. [Bearism No. 4.] If you can't solve a tough problem immediately, you have at least started on it, and you have put others on notice that it exists. People hate surprises, particularly big, ugly ones.

"Third, don't try to be the Lone Ranger. [Bearism No. 5.] We're a team, and we all have the same set of objectives. Our responsibility is to reach the best solution to each problem we can, *working together*. And when you go to someone to ask for help, don't be embarrassed or defensive. [Bearism No. 6.] You'll come across badly, and worse, you won't learn from the experience. I'll never criticize you for making a bad judgment or asking a stupid question when it's done in the context of asking for help. That goes for our office too. When we get stuck as a group, we ask our national office for help. When we sign a report, we sign The Firm, not our names as individuals.

"Now, there are going to be times when you'll feel worried or uncomfortable. One of those times will be when you're given an assignment and you aren't sure how to do it; you may feel like you're in over your head. Well, that's when you should rejoice, because it means you're making progress. [Bearism No. 7.] If you were doing the same thing over and over again, you'd be a clerk, not a professional; that's when you'd have cause to worry.

"And there will be times when you feel uncomfortable because you are being asked to do something you don't think is right. You may be asked by a client to do something that is against your best judgment, or a supervisor may ask you to take a shortcut or to tell a lie. I certainly hope that never happens in this office, but it could. This is when your sense of ethics comes into play. These are situations where you find out what kind of a person you really are. [Bearism No. 8.]

"The reason we hired you is that we believe in you and we're confident that you can handle new and challenging situations. We think you will handle the tough situations. We expect you to do the ethical thing. And we'll back you all the way, remembering, of course, that you're not the Lone Ranger."

The Bear then asked the shell-shocked group if anyone had questions for him. Nobody had anything profound to say, so we moved on to administration. We got a copy of a bunch of the bureaucratic stuff—staff manual, payroll forms, and the like. We also were given some technical manuals and assignment material for our firm's first training program, Group I School. We spent the rest of the morning on administrative things, had lunch with the partner in charge of our respective departments, attended to more administrative stuff, and then at 4:00 P.M. went to a reception with everybody in the office. One interesting question asked during our review of administrative matters was, What was the legal status of Firm manuals? We were told that they had significant legal standing. First, they represented certain commitments by The Firm to us—for example, regarding personnel policies. And second, when an accounting firm is sued for professional malpractice, its manuals were often subpoenaed to make sure they were complied with.

The idea of the reception was nice. The office was still small—fewer than fifty people. The Bear introduced each one of us by giving a little background, and then we met everybody personally. As corny as it might sound, we were like one big happy family.

Two weeks after my first day with The Firm, I was on a plane to Bromely Lake, Michigan, to attend Group I School at The Firm's national training center. Bromely Lake is a resort area 200 miles north of Lansing. The training center property had been acquired a number of years earlier, and the facility buildings were added as The Firm grew. The location is ideal for a summer program. The weather is good, and there are lots of fun things to do around the lake. The schedule for the program was rigorous but planned to allow us to take advantage of the resort environment and have a good time.

The program had two overriding objectives: to prepare us to begin work as new staff auditors and to make us feel like part of the larger firm. Each of us was assigned to a group with a group leader who was an audit manager. It was a privilege to be a group leader at this program, so the managers at the program were always among The Firm's best. My group leader was Mike Ensworth from the Kansas City office. Each member of the 15-person group was from a different office. We knew no one and the only things we had in common were our college training, our new employer, and being in the same group. The situation reminded me a little of some of my father's old army stories where circumstances produced strange bedfellows.

But, of course, The Firm had been running this program for years, and it was beautifully orchestrated. Soon, through the pleasure of social activities and the pain of a big audit case, we became fast friends and colleagues. We were in a competitive situation with the other groups, we were motivated and hard-charging professionals, and we idolized Mike Ensworth. We had a great time, and the six days passed very quickly. We said our good-byes at the airport, promising to be great friends for life.

Now I was back on the battlefront and ready to go to work. Our group had done well on the audit case, and I figured real audits couldn't be that tough, particularly since I was armed with all of The Bear's rules of behavior. Of course, I would soon find out that I didn't know all the rules yet and that there were many situations for which there are no rules.

When I got to the office, there was a message for me to contact Jed Wilkerson, who was in charge of scheduling. Jed had a big scheduling board on one wall of his office. This showed every professional's name down the side and his or her assignments over time, represented by columns. Scheduling a professional staff of any size is a demanding job. Jed used a computer program to assist in making the initial scheduling decisions. He discussed these decisions with various partners and managers, then posted the assignments on the board.

Jed welcomed me to his office. He was very friendly, and I remembered him from the orientation and reception. I think Jed tried to be well liked as a matter of style. People often got mad at him over scheduling decisions, when he was actually just the messenger in most cases. Jed gave me a nice smile and said, "Congratulations, Jack, you've been assigned to the Rineholt account." He handed me a piece of paper and said, "You need to call Jerry Lisbon at this extension." I knew this was good news, as Rineholt was the office's big account.

Rineholt Corporation is a publicly held conglomerate that has subsidiaries in construction, engineering, electronics, and cement manufacturing. Jerry Lisbon was the senior in charge of Cement. I didn't remember him from the reception, but he remembered me. He instructed me to meet him at 1:00 P.M. in the office he shared with another senior so that he could get me started on my first audit engagement.

When I saw Lisbon, his face was still not familiar, but that didn't get in the way of my liking him as soon as we met. He is a very tall fellow, about 6'5", and weighs less than I do. He had been a basketball player at San Francisco University. After I ate the first of many meals we shared together, I realized he ate more than any man I'd ever seen. But it didn't go to fat. I think Jerry just burned it up in support of the high energy level he maintained.

Jerry handed me a box full of workpaper files. "You, you lucky fellow, are going to be my new staff assistant on the Rineholt Cement audit. These are the permanent files. I want you to spend this afternoon and tomorrow studying them. On Wednesday, we're catching a plane to Bakersfield and we're going to rent a car and drive out to the Bakersfield plant. Janine is making the arrangements. We'll observe the inventory taking there and do some systems testing. Have you ever been to a cement plant?" I shook my head. "No? Well, then, you're in for a big thrill.

"Jack, the main thing I want you to do with these permanent files is to gain as good an understanding of how cement is made as you can. You'll hear The Bear say this a thousand times over your career: 'We audit the business, not the books.' [Bearism No. 9.] That means we have to understand the business. So learn as much about the business as you can. I'll be around, so ask me questions. When we get to the plant, you'll see everything first hand, and it will start to make sense. Oh, and one more thing, Jack—we'll wear suits down there, but be sure and bring a set of old work clothes. Okay?"

Was I getting dizzy? "Sure, okay, Jerry. It sounds great."

In school I had read about a lot of different businesses and I even saw the inside of an insurance company as part of our MBA field-study project, but going to the Bakersfield Cement Plant was a totally different experience. Cement plants are located near a source of cement's primary ingredient, limestone. The limestone is quarried and crushed into primary rock. This is sent by conveyor to the secondary and tertiary crushers nearer the plant. The tertiary rock is mixed with water and other chemicals into slurry, a liquid mud. This is run through the kiln, a rotating furnace hundreds of feet long. When the slurry emerges, it is a dried, crumbly substance called klinker. The klinker is ground in a final crushing process into fine cement. The cement is stored in silos for either bagging or bulk shipment.

On the flight down to the plant, Jerry told me that I would do the systems review and testing work, which involved payroll and some limited disbursement transactions, as well as physical inspection of fixed assets. Jerry would supervise me and do the inventory work. The company measured and valued the klinker and finished cement inventories. The whole thing should take us about three and a half days, meaning we'd work through Sunday morning and fly home on Sunday afternoon—just in time to get ready for work on Monday.

Things went well on Thursday and Friday. I got a chance to exercise my interviewing skills with the plant accounting people. In the MBA program, we had studied interviewing, and we practiced it in our big audit case at Group I School. I found that with my most pleasant, unassuming, and least intimidating behavior, the people I talked to were willing to answer my questions candidly and completely and to make sure I understood how their system worked. But, as Mike Ensworth had warned, it was clear that I was taking up time that the interviewees would rather be spending on something else. I did sense that as the people I was interviewing came to believe that I respected them and really was interested in the job they were doing, they became much more comfortable and really opened up.

One problem that occurred involved the clerk who handled miscellaneous cash receipts and who also was custodian for the plant's petty cash. The audit program I was using stated that after I reviewed the system over the receipts, I should test a small judgmental sample of transactions and count the petty cash fund to be certain that it was properly accounted for. I thanked the clerk for her explanation of how she handled transactions and then said I'd like to do the count.

The clerk balked and looked slightly distressed. "Well, sure, but I've just got to take care of one thing," she said, and pulled out her checkbook and wrote a check for $150 that she put in the petty cash box.

"I don't understand," I said. "What did you do that for?"

"Look, Jack. You seem like a nice guy. The fact is that I'm a single mother and sometimes I run a little short. If there's an emergency, I'll borrow a few dollars from petty cash. I always make it up, and it's never been a problem. I'd appreciate it if you'd just count the check as part of the fund."

"I'm sorry, Mrs. Glenn, I'm not sure I can do that. Does the company have a policy that deals with this?"

"I'm really not supposed to do it," she replied. She paused again and looked more distressed. She reached over and held my arm and said, "Jack, I think they might even fire me over this. You've got to help me out. Look, if you do, I promise I'll never do this again."

"Let me think about it," I said, and I went about counting the cash. It was all there, except for the check Mrs. Glenn had added.

I left Mrs. Glenn in a state of apprehension and went on to something else. Emotionally, I didn't want to be responsible for someone's getting fired. On the other hand, why would she be fired unless there were other problems as well? And besides, it wasn't my company, my problem, or my decision. At lunch I told Jerry what I had found and discussed my feelings about the situation with him.

"Good, Jack. You now know what it is to be one of the bad guys. Sometimes you have to give the client bad news and it's unpleasant, but when you think about it, we're not hired to tell the client everything's fine unless it really is. If there are any problems, we're expected to find them and tell the client about them. Then the client can deal with them in the way it thinks it should."

I never did find out what happened to Mrs. Glenn.

My biggest challenge on my first audit assignment came on Thursday afternoon when I was wrapping up testing a sample of disbursement transactions. I had finished the payroll work and was thinking we might finish up early and get home in time to enjoy a leisurely Sunday. Then Jerry came in to give me some news. "I just got a call from home, Jack. I've got some good news and some bad news. You want the good news first?"

"I guess so."

"The good news is that my other big client, Atrium Pharmaceuticals, has decided to merge with Belcon Products. Atrium will be the survivor and we'll get the combined work."

"That's great. What's the bad news?"

"The bad news is that we have to start a crash job to get the merger done, and I'm on my way back to Oakland right now. But there's more good news," he grinned. "You get to stay here and do the finished-cement inventory work tomorrow and Sunday morning. Harry will get you to the airport on time. Here's a set of instructions I've written for you to follow. Look them over and let's discuss them. Don't worry, Jack, I know you can handle this. You'll find out you know a lot more than you think you do." Jerry was on his way and I was in the exact position The Bear had described during orientation—in over my head.

The finished-cement inventory was in bulk form and in bags. The bulk cement was kept in silos and trucks, the bags in a storage building and also in trucks. Walt Emery was the finished-cement inventory manager at the plant and had overall responsibility for the count. On Saturday morning, his material handlers would count the bulk-loaded trucks and all the bags and record the counts on count sheets. I would observe the counts, make test counts, and get copies of the count sheets and receiving and shipping documents. We would check the computations back in Oakland where the cost accounting was done. On Saturday afternoon, Walt and I would go up to the top of the silos to measure the dead space in each silo with a long tape measure, and then we would use a chart to convert the measure into volume of cement. Everything went according to plan on Saturday morning. On Saturday afternoon, however, I ran into my second challenge.

The silos were about eighty feet high and twenty feet in diameter. Trucks drive to a device underneath the silos to receive a load of cement. To get to the top of the silo complex, I would have to ride a conveyorlike device with hand- and footholds. It's a little scary, but at least there's a protective housing around the conveyor. Walt reassured me by telling me that only one person had ever died trying to get to the top, and he'd been an internal auditor, so it didn't matter anyway. Walt's a funny guy.

On top of each silo there's a three-foot-square opening covered by a hatch. We lifted these off, dropped a weighted tape down into the darkness, shone a flashlight on it, and lifted it up and down a few times to be sure we were right on the surface of the cement. Walt showed me how to do this and let me practice and get the feel of it. It wasn't really too tough, and I felt like an expert in no time. When I was ready, we began. I measured the first silo and read off the tape to Walt: "Sixteen feet, four inches." Walt made the entry on his silo inventory sheet, but I noticed he wrote twelve feet, ten inches, instead of sixteen feet, four inches.

Walt noticed that I noticed and said, "Oh, there was one thing I forgot to tell you. When we do this, we have to take the dead-fill allowance factor into consideration."

"What's the 'dead-fill allowance factor'?" I asked.

"Well, it's impossible to fill these silos all the way to the top. The best you can do is get within three feet of the bottom of the hole here, and then you've got the six-inch lip for the hole itself. That means that from the point we're measuring, we have to subtract three and one-half feet to get the true reading."

I wasn't in a position to know whether this was right or wrong, so we just went on with the measurements. But it just didn't seem reasonable to me. If some factor were required, wouldn't it be built into the conversion charts instead of being left up to the knowledge and judgment of the person making the measurements? When I got back to the plant office, I asked the plant engineer if he had drawings of the silos. He did. I took the detailed drawing of the first silo and got the precise dimensions of the inside of the silo. I used these to compute volume and made a few conversions with hypothetical measurements from the top. I did these both with and without Walt's factor. I compared my results with the conversion table and found that the conversion table was correct when the allowance factor was ignored.

Great, two problems in two days—only this one was a lot bigger than the check in petty cash, and there was no Jerry around to talk to. I firmed up my resolve and went to see Harry Lemley, the plant manager. When I explained the situation to Harry, he became very concerned. "You're absolutely right about this, Jack. I appreciate that you found this and came to see me about it. I think I know the problem. Walt is a great guy and an extremely loyal and conscientious employee. He takes great pride in his work. I noticed that our finished-cement shortage number was getting somewhat out of hand a few months ago, and then it just reversed. Walt was embarrassed by it and, in his mind, it was making him look bad. I think Walt was reversing it by adjusting the inventory numbers. I'll talk to him and get the situation corrected. You've got your inventory numbers there so you can check to make sure the right ones are sent in."

I left Bakersfield feeling that I had not only learned a lot but had done a good job as well.

Discussion Questions

5–1 Explain the meaning of "public" in the title Certified Public Accountant.

5–2 Describe your view of the "ideal culture" for an office of a CPA firm.

5–3 How important is firm training to you, and just what do you expect?

5–4 How important are client assignments to one's professional development and advancement? Explain.

5–5 *What are the keys to conducting an effective interview?*

5–6 *Should an auditor be concerned with minor peculations such as the "borrowing" of petty cash illustrated in this chapter? How should this matter have been dealt with by the petty cash custodian's supervisor?*

5–7 *How do Jack's experiences at the cement plant illustrate (a) the need to understand a client's business and (b) the concept of professional skepticism?*

6

We Are Family

Being in public accounting is a little like being a farmer. The months are different, but the seasons are clear. Work gets done by the calendar—there is a busy time followed by a time of recovery, rededication, and renewal. The busy season runs from about January 15, when the bulk of the work on calendar-year audit clients starts, through April 15, the end of tax season. After the busy season, there are always a number of staff members who decide it's time to make a shift into corporate accounting, private practice, or some other endeavor. These people leave, and then about July 1, a new crop of fresh young faces is added to the staff through college recruiting. The summer is spent taking vacations, training, planning for upcoming audits, doing interim work, and conducting engagements for non–calendar-year clients. Then winter comes and it starts all over again.

My first six months with The Firm were exciting and enjoyable. I liked the work because it allowed me to focus on and complete specific tasks. And I particularly liked being part of an active social structure. When I returned from Bakersfield, I found there was a social process that was going on in the office and I jumped right in. Because the office was relatively small, everyone was very close, all the way from The Bear down to the mailboy, and including spouses and significant others. Friday nights set the tone.

There was a bar in the lower level of the Merritt Plaza Building called Elmo's. Elmo was a real character, as was his wife, Amy. In their younger days, Elmo and Amy were in show business. They had lived back east and performed a song and dance act in resorts in the Catskills. Most of us who were in the office or within reasonable commuting distance would meet at Elmo's after work on Friday nights. Our spouses or dates would join us. We would talk to Elmo and Amy about things in our lives and theirs and about all the other things in the world. Elmo had an extra bartender come in about six, and he and Amy would move over to the piano and we'd all sing Broadway show tunes. Elmo's didn't serve dinner, but it had great *hors d'oeuvres*. By about eight we had solved all the world's problems and reset The Firm on a proper course, so we'd set off for the weekend, alone or in groups. A bunch of us were still single, so we would go to dinner, a show, or another club. I was definitely leading the good life.

In addition to Friday nights at Elmo's, we had our softball team. All the accounting firms in the East Bay belonged to a recreational softball league. We had two teams, the "pros" and the rest of us. The pros played fast pitch and got fairly serious. The rest of us played in the class D, mixed soft-pitch competition. Because of my gimpy leg, I couldn't run well enough to play with the pros, so I was on the soft-pitch team. We were serious too, but only about having a good time. We played softball all summer, one or two nights a week. Those who didn't play came and rooted. After the games, we met at a beer and pizza place in the Oakland foothills and either celebrated or commiserated. We had a wonderful time and became very close. I can understand why those who left The Firm always expressed their regrets in a very sincere way.

In September, The Bear hosted the annual golf outing, held at his country club. My first year at The Firm was the first year women participated. In previous years, only the men played. The women were placated by being given a gift certificate and a "shopping day." As more women joined our professional staff, there were complaints that this practice was unfair and discriminatory. Women were at a disadvantage in business in terms of their opportunity to network with men. The old-boys club and business on the golf course were two things that were beginning to change. Bear made the decision that our women professionals, none of whom were partners, needed to be better supported and, among other things, included them in the outing.

Whereas I wasn't much as far as softball goes, I was in my element on the golf course. I had two special goals for my first year with The Firm. One was to pass the CPA examination in my first sitting, which would be in November. The second was to have the low gross score at the golf outing. I had been sizing up the competition and figured there were only one or two guys in the office who could shoot in the 70s. Then I found out about Millie Truett. It turns out that Millie had gone to Cal State on a golf scholarship. She was a scratch handicap. I was a dead man. Not only would I probably not win, I would lose to a woman. But what a woman. When I saw Millie hit a golf ball, all I could do was tip my hat in admiration. And she was as gracious in victory as I was in defeat: "Keep working on your game, Jackie boy, and someday I might let you caddie for me." But I got my revenge. I won four bucks from her playing bridge later in the evening.

One of the highlights of the outing was the barbecue after we finished playing golf. There were beer and steaks, chicken and ribs, corn—the whole works. As we were all finishing our dinners, I found out about another tradition, the annual Skip Greene poem. It seems that Skip, who was the unofficial nickname giver in the office, spent a good deal of time each year cataloging the minor successes and foibles of people in the firm. He would then present these in the form of a humorous poem that he read at the golf outing each year. This year's poem was hilarious, particularly a line that included the words *bear*, *lair*, *glare*, *fair*, *hair*, *mare*, *snare*, and *dare*. The Bear enjoyed this more than anyone. You could see how he had a sense of the group's spirit, something he tried very hard to maintain.

The final big social event of the year was the Christmas party. This was also held at The Bear's club, but upstairs in the main dining room. It was formal and first class. There was a reception and cocktails followed by a full-course dinner with good wine, a band, and dancing. There was also a performance by the Good Ol' Boys. One of the staff, Tim Bellows, had worked his way through college as a folk singer. He had assembled three other staff members to form a folksinging group. When the band took a long break, Tim and his group sang the old classic folk songs, and everyone gathered and sang along.

I guess as a bachelor, I felt somewhat self-conscious, and I wanted to make a good impression at the party. I planned to rent an Armani tux and to invite Carolyn Benchley, the most beautiful woman I knew. I called Carolyn, and unfortunately, she was busy. I called the next best on my list and had no luck there either. As I was pondering what to do next, Don Parnell came into my cubicle and asked if I was up for lunch. When I told him my problem, he said, "That reminds me—Dee Dee has this sorority sister, Libby Ellingsen, who she thinks would really hit it off with you. Do you think you might want to invite her to the Christmas party?"

"I don't know, Don, I'm not big on blind dates." The fact is, I am always a little uncomfortable about having a limp. After I get to know someone well, it doesn't bother me, but it does at first.

"I can guarantee you that you won't be disappointed in Libby. She's down-to-earth and good looking too. She's an elementary school teacher. I know you'll like her. Why don't we set up a dinner at our place to introduce you, then you can decide whether to invite her to the Christmas party for yourself."

"All right, but can we do it soon? I'm starting to panic. I really don't want to go to this party by myself."

The rest is history. Libby and I dated a little bit during the busy season, and when it was over, we saw a lot of each other. When the following summer came, Libby and another of her girlfriends spent two months in Europe. The effect of her absence was to make us both realize that we were in love. We got engaged and were married the following December—just in time for the next Christmas party and the following busy season.

I spent November through March working on the Rineholt audit. During the first week of November, The Bear, who was the engagement partner for Rineholt, convened everyone working on the job for a planning meeting. Actually, the planning had been done, and this was where all of us were brought into the picture. Bear said that overall, Rineholt was having a pretty good year but that there were some problems in construction and electronics.

These were both divisions that did contract work on a fixed-fee basis, so there was a risk of our suffering large losses on contracts that weren't bid well or where unforeseen problems occurred. Rineholt had good management and good controls. Management had given fairly optimistic earnings forecasts all year, and The Bear was worried they might have backed themselves into a corner. He wanted us to keep our skepticism about us throughout the audit. He liked to say that healthy skepticism means that if we aren't skeptical, we're risking *our* professional health. [Bearism No. 10.]

Bear cautioned us to be sure to do two things: Never audit by "conversation," and always put things to the "reasonableness test." [Bearisms 11 and 12.] He elaborated on the first point by simply pointing out that most of the client people from whom we would get representations have a strong vested interest in a high earnings number. They are naturally biased, even if they are very honest people. We need to get as much "hard" evidence as we can and rely solely on representations only when there is no other choice.

Bear then surprised the heck out of me by telling everyone about my experience on the silos of Bakersfield as an illustration of a reasonableness test. "Look and think," he said. "Be skeptical. Make sure *you* understand. Check it out. Be satisfied before you let go."

Someone asked about the problem of running up too much time doing what may be "extra steps." Bear responded by explaining that his approach to an engagement was always to ignore the fee once it had been agreed upon with the client and to focus entirely on doing a good audit. [Bearism No. 13.] "I'm the partner and I'm responsible for the fee and the quality of our work. I want the client to be happy and I want to sleep well after I sign 'The Firm' on the audit report. You folks are my backup. We can pile a mountain of review on top of a pinhead of work, and in the final analysis, we're still relying on each of you to do a good job. [Bearism No. 14.] That's what I'm asking each of you to do."

He ended up by admonishing the managers and seniors on the job to ensure that they paid attention to on-the-job development of the staff under their supervision. He said that one of the major pitfalls of supervising others is to try to save time by cutting back on on-the-job training. He said that time spent on planning and on-the-job training always pays off. [Bearism No. 15.]

Finally, he talked to the junior staff members about taking responsibility for our own development. He said that we should not only expect but also demand development help from our supervisors. At the same time, we had to make sure we understood what we were doing and why we were doing it. If we kept our mouths shut because we were embarrassed to admit our ignorance by asking questions, then we'd just stay ignorant. He also said to be sure to challenge whether what we were instructed to do was the right thing to do and the best way to do it. He stated that just because something was done a certain way last year doesn't mean that it was done right. [Bearism No. 16.] We all had a responsibility for continuous improvement of the audit.

As I had expected, most of the work I did during that first year was of a pretty low level. But that was okay—I could handle it and think about what I was doing and why I was doing it all at the same time. My feeling that I had things under control made the transition from school into practice manageable. In school, most of the problems and cases we had were at a management level; I was doing specific functional tasks in practice. And in the problems and cases we had, the information was always neatly parceled. Here, I often had to find out what information was available and where and how I could get it.

One of the things I discovered was the importance of organizational and administrative skills. I would be given a task and it would always involve deciding the best way to do it. I'd have to talk to client people and get them to agree to do something for me. I'd have to look at assets or documents or to make computations. I'd have to document what I did and what I found, then communicate everything upward to Jerry, the manager, and the partner in a way that was clear, concise, and time-saving to them. If I found problems, I would have to consider what the implications were on the audit and whether a recommendation to the client should be made.

This process involved planning, communication, workpaper design, and tasks such as using the computer and the copying machine. The term "cut and paste" took on a new meaning. The office had just begun to use microcomputers in its practice. We had one for Cement, and we were encouraged to type audit memos documenting our work and findings. I found that my typing skills were suddenly very important. Things were clearly more "practical" in practice than they had been in school.

We also had to keep track of the things we did in terms of time spent. The job was controlled by an engagement budget that showed the time we expected to spend completing each major area of the audit, who would do the work in each area, and when they would do it. Each day, I would summarize my time by audit area and enter it onto a detailed workpaper we had for accumulating time. At the end of the week, before we were off to Elmo's, Jerry would enter the time for the week on a summary sheet. We would then discuss how much time it would take to finish the areas we were working on. If it looked as though we were spending too much time in an area, we would discuss the reasons why. Where it was clear that the reason related to the client and not to our ineptitude, Jerry would pass that information on up to the engagement manager so that it could enter into fee discussions.

We would also each enter our total time by client on semi-monthly timesheets. These would be approved by Jerry and sent into the office with any supporting expense documentation. The semi-monthly timesheets were the basis for our paychecks as well as billings to clients. Timesheet data are also the basis for operating statistics and reports on staff time utilization. The Firm calculated the percentage of chargeable time to standard available time by professionals and used that information to judge the adequacy of staff levels, relative profitability, and individual staff performance. The problem with this measure, of course, is that in one sense it motivates inefficiency rather than efficiency, as the higher your utilization rate is, the better you look.

One of the other new staff persons on the Cement audit besides me was a second-year man named Arthur Pringle. In November and December, we were working the client's hours, 8:30 A.M. to 5:00 P.M., with an hour for lunch. During one of our weekend planning meetings, Jerry asked Arthur why he charged eight hours each day to the engagement on his timesheet when we were working only seven and one-half. Arthur looked surprised at Jerry's question. "I'm responsible for charging a full day every day," said Arthur. "I'm not about to take a hit on my utilization rate just because Cement doesn't work a normal eight-hour day. Besides, Barnes said not to worry about fee-related stuff."

I thought Jerry was going to choke. "Do you mean you think we should charge our clients for work we don't do?"

"Well, lawyers do it, don't they?" Arthur responded. I watched Arthur digging himself into a hole.

"What about the time charged on the engagement summary, Arthur?"

"Oh, I only charged seven and one-half hours on the worksheet. I wasn't going to overstate how long it takes me to do the audit steps."

Jerry glared at Arthur. Then he finally said, "Arthur, if you *ever* misrecord your time again, for any reason, in any way, I'll have your tail. Do you understand me?"

"Well, yes, Jerry. Gosh, you don't have to get so excited."

Then an unexpected thing happened a couple of days later. Jerry came in and told me that Arthur Pringle was leaving the firm and that a new hire was joining the engagement team. Furthermore, I would be doing some of Arthur's tasks and I would even supervise the new hire to some extent. I asked if Arthur had been fired because of the timesheet incident. Jerry told me that Arthur hadn't been fired, he'd quit, but that The Bear didn't try and talk him out of leaving.

The new hire's name was Sheldon Mitchell. Sheldon had attended FSU and had gone through the recruiting process at the same time I had, only he did not have a graduate degree. Sheldon had gone to work for a small corporation as its controller. About six months into the job, Sheldon was reviewing the previous year's income tax returns to get ready to prepare the current year's returns. He noticed that the amount shown for inventory on the return was much lower than he'd expected. When he asked the business's owner about this, he was told that the inventory on the return was determined using "poor man's LIFO." In other words, it was a bogus number entered to reduce taxable income. Sheldon told his boss that it was against IRS regulations to value the inventory that way and that he wouldn't prepare or sign a return that contained false figures. Sheldon's boss said he understood and wished Sheldon well in his search for new employment. When Wally Garner heard

44

about this, he called The Bear to see if we needed anyone. We did, and Sheldon was hired.

One of Arthur's planned assignments was to audit Cement's shipping subsidiary. In addition to cement manufacturing, Cement had a gypsum-mining operation on an island off the coast of Mexico. The gypsum was simply scraped off the surface of this island, ground up, and fed into the holds of two ships that were owned and operated by Shipping. The neat thing about working on the audit of Shipping was that I got to do the whole thing from beginning to end, not just pieces of a larger entity. (Bearism No. 17.) This was extremely satisfying to me. I reviewed the permanent file, read about shipping, learned new terminology, talked with operations people about how things worked, reviewed Shipping's systems, reviewed and revised the audit program, and performed and documented all the tests.

One of the more interesting, and I guess humorous, aspects of Shipping was the naming of their two ships. One was the *Oswaldo Pedilla,* and the other was the *Guillermo Garrezar.* I asked one of the operating people if those were the names of Mexican heroes. "Not exactly, Jack. Those are the names of the two attorneys in Mexico who 'facilitated' our getting the mining rights on San Fellipe Island. I guess in that sense they're heroes to us." I got it. Back in the fifties when Cement began the gypsum operation, the only way it could get these rights was to "buy" them. The Foreign Corrupt Practices Act, passed in the 1970s, clearly made this kind of thing illegal, and we wouldn't expect to see it happen again.

Given the size of Shipping, the simplicity of its operations, and its size relative to Cement on a consolidated basis, I figured I would audit the accounts at year end, rather than try to rely on and test controls. This would involve going to Long Beach, where the gypsum was unloaded, to inspect the ships and test the inventory being carried. In this case, inventory included not only Cement's gypsum but also the ships' bunker fuel oil. This was definitely another "old clothes" job. When I talked to Jerry about my plan, he agreed, but he told me to request someone from the Los Angeles office to do the observation work. It didn't make sense for me to fly to L.A. to do something someone in that office could do just as well.

The Firm had specific policies and procedures for referring work to other offices. These were laid out in the practice manual I had been given. I found I was able to learn and manage this new challenge with no difficulty. However, I still called and talked to the Los Angeles office and the staff member assigned the work. I wanted to be absolutely sure my first "complete" audit went off without any problems.

In addition to managing my engagement tasks and responsibilities during my first busy season, I had to manage my life. This wasn't bad in November and December, when my major concern was taking and passing the CPA exam. After talking to Wally, I figured that I could clearly distinguish myself by passing the entire exam on my first sitting; there were so few who managed to do that. So I developed a strategy to pass the exam: I took a CPA review course, read a law section review book three times (this convinced me that my decision not to go to law school was a good one), memorized the ten generally accepted auditing standards, and read Statements of Financial Accounting Standards and did problems in consolidations and other more complicated areas for hours on end. I took the exam and felt that I had done well on all four parts.

It's a good thing the exam is in November, because as we got well into the busy period, it became more and more difficult to deal with meals, paying bills, getting my laundry done, and maintaining some semblance of a personal life.

Then, just as things were winding down at Rineholt, I got a call to come into the office to see Jed. Jed informed me that there was a problem in the Denver office and that Oakland and San Francisco had been asked to send six staff members there to help out. It seems that the Denver office had merged with a local firm that had a large tax practice. Unfortunately, the ex–managing partner of the merged firm died. He apparently had possession of the files for about 300 tax clients, and the files had disappeared. Furthermore, most of the merged firm's staff had left The Firm. The office was able to reconstruct a client list from billing records and was in the process of contacting all of these clients. This had caused an unbelievable mess, and six "loaners" were needed to get the return preparation done.

My golfing buddy Millie and I flew to Denver from Oakland on March 23. We and the other loaners—we called ourselves "The California Crash Team"—were all auditors, rather than tax people. The tax staff was busy doing tax work of its own. Our first four days were spent in a special training session to teach us how to prepare federal and Colorado returns. Some of us who had not yet filed our own returns filed a request for extension, as we would be too busy to worry about our own returns now.

We worked 12 hours a day for six days a week, plus a half day on Sunday—a total of 76 hours. We worked in a staff room that had no windows. We had most of our meals sent in. I have to admit that it was an interesting experience. Not only did I develop good tax skills, but I also improved my level of patience, tolerance, and understanding. Working so many hours in such small quarters for such a long period of time caused the California Crash Team to really get on one another's nerves from time to time. By April 15, I was so punchy and sick of the inside of that work space that I would have done anything to get out of there. On the night of the fifteenth, the Denver office threw a big going-away party for us. We flew back to Oakland on the sixteenth, having each worked 236 hours in 23 days.

I realized that I had now had the experience of the busy season. It had been stimulating and rewarding in many ways. The experience had also been tiring and at some times frustrating. But spring had arrived and things began to look rosy again. Had I liked my first year? Overall, yes. Did I want to keep going down this path? Certainly; I felt I was doing well, I got good feedback, I had learned a lot about auditing and about the cement and shipping businesses, and I would have more responsibility and learn a lot more during my second year. I had made more money than I'd ever seen before because of all the overtime, and I hadn't spent much of it because I was too busy. Furthermore, the trip to Denver resulted in a special bonus, which I used to help buy a new car. I also met my goal of passing the CPA exam. It was definitely a go for year two.

Discussion Questions

6–1 What are the effects on an accounting practice and practitioners of the "busy season"?

6–2 How important are social events in managing an accounting practice?

6–3 Which is more important in the long run, good in-house training programs or effective on-the-job training? Explain.

6–4 What administrative skills must a CPA acquire?

6–5 Time budgets are said to have both functional and dysfunctional effects. What are they?

6–6 Thoreau said that we should be careful to avoid overimplementing the concept of division of labor. How might this advice apply to conducting an audit?

6–7 What special problems occur when work is referred to another office?

6–8 How important is it for a new staff member to pass the CPA exam? Explain.

6–9 In reviewing Jack Butler's first year with The Firm, would you say his travel has been too little, too much, or about what you would expect?

7

The Growth Years

My first year with The Firm was a time of discovery, about The Firm and about the auditing profession in general; my next three years were years of tremendous personal and professional growth. By my second year, I had gotten to know everyone pretty well, and I was no longer on the bottom rung of the corporate ladder. The hierarchy of a CPA firm is clear, although there are some differences in titles from firm to firm. At The Firm, one starts out as a new staff assistant, moves to experienced staff assistant in year two, and then on to light senior, senior, heavy senior, manager, senior manager, and finally partner. The time in the manager positions varies the most, and it generally takes between ten and twelve years to achieve partnership. Along the way, people drop out for various reasons. Some just tire of the rigors of the profession, others leave for better opportunities, and some are counseled out. Until recently, The Firm, like the other large firms, had a fairly strict "up-or-out" policy. Each year staff members were evaluated and either received a promotion or were advised that it was time to seek other opportunities. This was generally done with some sensitivity, because many firm alumni went with clients, and those who went with nonclients were viewed as a source of new business.

The up-or-out system was well understood and accepted. But a couple of times over the years it has been violated by some firms that executed wholesale cutbacks. One blatant and costly example occurred in The Firm's New York office during my second year. The office overhired the previous summer and, after the busy season, realized it was way overstaffed going into the less busy time of year. The office's management decided to "unhire" 20 percent of its new staff assistants. Office management drew lots to determine which staff members would be released, believing this to be the "most equitable" method available. It turned out, unbeknownst to office management, that one of the lottery winners was the daughter of the chief financial officer of a major New York bank. When the father found out about the treatment of his daughter, he undertook against The Firm a campaign that hurt it for several years.

During my first few years, our office was growing at an average annual rate of about 10 percent. This meant that each year, with normal turnover, four or five people would leave and seven or eight new people would be added. Because most of the people who left had been with the firm for four to six years, there was great opportunity for advancement for lower-level staff. My progress in The Firm was accelerated by the incident with Andy Pringle on the Rineholt audit. In effect, I got boosted through the staff assistant level and was acting as a light senior by the end of my second year. This gave me some early experience supervising others on Rineholt, and it led to other assignments at the light senior level.

As a supervising person, I had several responsibilities that were particularly important. One was delegating work effectively. The main idea is to make sure both parties communicate effectively and are clear on the terms of the delegation. Believe it or not, there are whole books on the art of delegation, answering such questions as: How much responsibility and authority are being delegated? When should the delegatee ask questions? How often should the delegatee report in? And, what output at each stage of the job does the delegator expect?

The second important responsibilities were review and on-the-job training. Jerry Lisbon was a master at this and taught me well. Jerry went over everything and anything I did on his jobs in great detail. He would call me in, give me his written comments, explain the basis of each comment, and then, after he was sure I understood them, he would send me back to my workspace to make all the corrections he indicated. Then at the end of each week, he'd ask me, "What did you learn this week, Jack?" and I'd have to tell him. Another thing Jerry did was to include me in as many meetings with client personnel as possible. He intended to expose me to higher-level client personnel and give me a first-hand idea of how these meetings are handled. Jerry's efforts took a lot of time, but they caused me to develop my skills at light speed. I tried to pay Jerry back by working hard for him and then giving the same effort to my charges.

Finally, there were the staff evaluation forms. This is the process all CPA firms of any size use to give formal feedback to staff. At The Firm, a formal evaluation is required on every assignment of forty hours or more. The evaluation is prepared in writing on a specified form by the person's immediate supervisor, then discussed with the person evaluated. There is space for the expression of disagreement by the person evaluated, and the form is signed by both parties. It is then passed on to the person's personnel file, where it is used again during the staff member's annual evaluation.

Basically, the evaluator summarizes the strengths and weaknesses the person has displayed on the job. When we were trained on preparing the staff evaluation forms, we were warned to be as objective as possible. There are a couple of problems that objectivity is intended to overcome. One is that we all want to be "nice guys"; it is always easier to say something nice about people than to have to confront them with criticism. But it doesn't help anyone to gloss over problems. The second problem is that if we were overly negative—or overly positive—and the personnel file is subpoenaed as part of a lawsuit, our lack of objectivity could be used against us.

Because of the effort the office put into recruiting, we had good staff with few exceptions, and the evaluations were generally positive. I found that where I did make a negative comment, the downside impact of it could be mitigated by offering advice and assistance on overcoming the criticism.

Most of my second-year busy season was spent on the Rineholt audit, on the Cement and Shipping divisions, but I did some work on the Electronics division as well. Working on Electronics was extremely interesting to me because it was "high tech" manufacturing, and I was able to learn about a type of automated production process that was becoming widely used throughout industry. After the busy season was over, at the beginning of my third year, one of the best things that happened during the earlier years of my career occurred. I was assigned to the Frazier Manufacturing Company audit.

As with all large firms, the bulk of The Firm's fees came from its large, publicly held clients, but the bulk of its clients in number were actually smaller businesses. Furthermore, the large firms cultivate small-business clients for a number of reasons. First, they are a major source of tax consulting and financial planning work, and second, small companies grow to become large companies.

The big problem with having small-company clients is that they are more sensitive to staff turnover than are large companies. Small companies perceive that there is a cost associated with constantly "breaking in" new staff people. They also like to develop a more personal relationship with their accountants, and such a relationship is disrupted by turnover. So, providing continuity in a business like public accounting that has a high turnover rate is important and tricky. Some firms approach this problem by having a separate small-business department. The Firm tried this for a while and then disbanded it. It found that turnover in the small-business department was also a problem, and worse, small-business department personnel were often considered second-class citizens. The Bear's solution in our office was to pick a second- or third-year person on the staff who he believed would be around for the next three years and to assign him or her to the client on a "3-year deal." The arrangement included a commitment to the client that the staff person would be its man or woman for the next three years, and that the fee for those years would be fixed. The Bear argued that this was a win-win-win approach. The client got continuity and controlled cost, The Firm got a happy and continuing client, and the assigned staff person got the experience of working on all facets of an engagement in the small-client environment. Frazier Manufacturing turned out to be my favorite client.

Frazier Manufacturing was a high-grade furniture and fixture manufacturer. Its primary customers were banks and brokerage offices in northern

California that wanted public spaces that were both functional and impressive. The company had the ability to conceive, design, manufacture, and install such spaces. They were works of art, and the company's owner, Wilson Frazier, was the master artist. His employees were all craftsmen. From the first day I set foot on the premises, I was fascinated by the talent and ability that Frazier's people demonstrated. I loved to see the special woods and how they were worked into beautiful pieces, and I loved to talk with Wilson Frazier about these processes.

Wilson Frazier was clearly a gentleman of the old school. He was then in his early sixties, had snow-white hair, and came to work every day dressed impeccably in a suit. After he arrived, he would change into "work clothes"—tweed slacks and a sweater. He generally lunched with friends, or with existing or potential customers, for which he would "re–suit up." His manners were exemplary. His weakness, if it was one, was his habit of talking about the early days of his business when craftsmen were more abundant and seemed to care more about the quality of their work and less about fringe benefits.

One of Wilson's primary employees was Martha O'Leary, his bookkeeper. Martha ran the office in the tradition of Attila the Hun. She intimidated every salesperson (and auditor) who crossed her path and demanded total obedience of the company's policies and procedures from employees. Wilson loved it that way. Martha was the bad-guy foil to his Mr. Good Guy.

Wilson and Quentin Barnes had been friends for years. The Firm's audit of Frazier Manufacturing facilitated its bank debt and bonding ability. The Firm did the company's tax returns and all of Wilson's tax planning and tax work. The Firm was more costly than a local firm would be, but Wilson liked to "do things right." Quentin was committed to making sure that Wilson got the service he deserved, which put a certain amount of positive pressure on me in serving Wilson as a client.

When I got the assignment, The Bear gave me the background on the company and on Wilson Frazier. The Bear wanted me to do as much of the tax work myself as I could, using the tax department as a backup if necessary. He told me to put my MBA to work and to try to come up with an extra-good management letter during the next audit. He also told me that the auditor I was succeeding had done okay but had never really established a rapport with Wilson, let alone with Martha O'Leary. Fortunately, Barbara Gillespie had done some special tax work for Wilson and his company, and they loved her.

As it turned out, I hit it off with Wilson and also with Martha. Wilson had known my uncle Dave at San Francisco University during their college days. Wilson hadn't seen Dave in years and enjoyed hearing about him. I was able to get them together to become reacquainted when Dave came to visit over the holidays.

With Martha, the hook was my ability to help her solve some problems she was having with the company's new computer system. She was receiving terrible service from the vendor of the system. I was familiar with it from another client situation and was able to help her out without too much trouble. I also made a point to show Martha great deference, making sure to ask her for help, rather than telling her things I might think she didn't know.

So I learned the fine furniture and cabinetmaking business, got to see and feel exotic hardwoods, smell varnish and glue, and got to design and conduct an audit, do tax work, and spend time with the client's owner and CEO. When it came to making recommendations, I was also able to help the company. The reason Wilson had ordered the new computer system was that he felt he needed more and better information with which to manage his company. When he told me about that, it opened the door for a discussion about what criteria he should use in deciding what information to maintain. I had been impressed with readings in graduate school about critical success factors (the four or five things most important to the ultimate success of a business). I dug up some references on that approach for Wilson to read. He was also impressed, and asked me to help design CSFs into his system.

As part of the audit, of course, I reviewed the company's internal controls. It was fairly obvious that Martha had so much to do with all aspects of the accounting system that she was in a position to steal Wilson blind if she wanted to. I discussed this with The Bear, and he told me that he had discussed it with Wilson from time to time. Wilson told him that Martha had been with him from the start, and if he couldn't trust her, then "just what the hell was life all about?" The Bear, said there has never been any indication that Martha was not an honest and loyal employee. He said that we shouldn't push this as an issue, but that we should do tests of transactions in areas of the greatest exposure, even though we were doing essentially a substantive audit.

I enjoyed my three years working with Wilson and Martha. I'm glad I never found anything of great concern. I became very fond of them and they of me. They weren't a "company," some faceless legal entity represented by products and marketing campaigns; they were two wonderful people whose professional relationship and personal friendship came to mean a lot to me. Wilson retired two years after I rotated off the job, and he died of heart failure a short time later. The Bear and I and our wives went to Wilson's funeral and were grateful to have known him.

As my third year progressed, I focused my personal development efforts in the computer area. It had become clear that microcomputers were here to stay. Not only were we using personal computers more and more in our practice, but clients were using smaller systems for their accounting and information purposes, and "shadow systems" were showing up around Rineholt. For example, in Cement's shipping company, the cost accountant had written a spreadsheet program that analyzed bunker fuel oil usage under differing circumstances to try to get better control over fuel costs.

I figured that if I could get up to speed with computers, I would have a competitive advantage in The Firm and with my clients. After my experience with Frazier Manufacturing, I also hoped I could put myself in a position to work on some consulting engagements, many of which involved computer systems. So late in the summer, I approached The Bear and asked if I could go to an extra training program on small-business computer systems. One was being offered in the first week of September, before things got too busy at Rineholt. I threw in my willingness to forgo any vacation if that would help.

The Bear gave me The Smile and asked me what this was all about. I told him my thoughts and intentions, and he agreed it was probably a good use of my time. He said I could go. Then he turned to the topic of consulting from a different point of view.

"Jack, if you want to do consulting, you should first think in terms of the skills you already have—your minor in statistics."

Hello in there. I thought, *What an idiot!* I got out of school with all this statistical knowledge, which I took because I thought I could use it, and then I forgot all about it after I started to work.

The Bear was still talking. "A number of years ago The Firm started a formal statistical sampling effort. We hired a professor to consult with us. We developed materials for attribute sampling and dollar-unit sampling, and, as you know, we use them on a lot of our jobs. But we also trained a core of people in the use of a bunch of advanced methods. We had a fellow here who was our office statistical coordinator. I guess the program lost its momentum and was eventually scrapped when firm management changed. Right now, I don't think there are any statistical coordinators left in the firm.

"There could be an opportunity for you here, Jack. I'll contact the Sacramento, San Francisco, and San Jose offices and tell them we have a real statistical guru here in Oakland, and if they have any special statistical needs, they should contact me. I'll screen what comes in and set you up to do the work. We'll see how it goes, and if it goes well, we can turn it into something a little more organized."

So that's how I got to do some consulting. About a month later, The Bear told me he had been contacted by Harvey Bendell, the partner in charge of the San Jose office, who needed some statistical assistance. Bear told me to call Harvey and take it from there.

Harvey was the partner responsible for a number of the San Jose office's larger clients. One of them was a discount chain that served both northern and southern California by the name of Everything's Here, Inc. Harvey and his staff were wrestling with a couple of problems related to EHI's inventory. First, they had to observe it as part of the audit. The inventory was located at three distribution centers and eighty-seven different stores, all generally the same size and configuration. The inventory could be described as a set of several thousand standard product codes. Each distribution center supported 90 percent of the codes, and each store at any one point in time contained up to 60 percent of the codes. Harvey intended to observe inventory at all three distribution centers and wanted to take a statistical approach to visiting and observing inventory at the stores.

The solution to this first problem was to design a two-stage sample. The first stage was a random sample of stores to visit, and the second stage was a random sample of specific product codes to check in each store. There were a couple of practical problems here caused by a lack of information about the store inventories and by the fact that all stores wouldn't contain all products. In order to resolve these, we visited five stores just to gather preliminary information. Once that was obtained, it was relatively easy to design the sampling plan.

The second problem to solve for EHI was to determine a way to use statistical sampling to determine economically its inventory on a LIFO basis. The company, wanting to know its latest inventory costs, kept its detailed inventory records on a FIFO basis but used LIFO for tax and reporting purposes, since it was expanding and could defer a significant tax liability that way. The IRS followed the practice of allowing companies to compute their LIFO index based on sampling; however, it held companies to a fairly high level of statistical precision and reliability.

In solving the inventory observation problem, we were constrained by the fact that we had to send auditors to observe the inventory taking. This required us to minimize the number of stores we visited to keep costs under control. For the LIFO conversion, however, we could easily gather information from every store by simply having the client's employees do it. So for that purpose, I designed a random sample of product code by store, considering the distribution centers as stores. We printed up worksheets for the sample product codes grouped by store. We sent them to each store, where the count and value information as of the inventory date was filled in. The worksheets were returned to the San Jose office, where we tested the information and computed the LIFO index. The total sample size was less than a thousand items throughout the entire company. In a subsequent IRS examination I was asked to discuss the approach with the examining agent, and he thought it was fine.

Bendell was so impressed with my work on EHI that he posed another problem to me. It seemed that one of his public clients, Henshaw Controls, was undertaking an effort in the defense business by manufacturing instruments used in missile systems. Miles Henshaw was the grandson of the company's founder and held a sizeable block of stock, although not one big enough to give him control of the company. Miles had decided to make an issue of the defense strategy at the forthcoming stockholders' meeting. He had put forth several "peace issues" and was trying to have at least one board member replaced. Company management was concerned that if Miles's issues were defeated, he would claim that the proxy count was rigged. It's true that a representative from the agency that handles the proxies would be there, but management wanted The Firm to be involved in order to add even more credibility to the process.

Harvey and I came up with a plan whereby we would independently verify the proxy count. We would take a random sample of proxies and get direct verification of their authenticity and accuracy. We would report our findings directly to the chairman of the board. The primary concern was to be sure that the statistical precision and reliability were beyond reproach. We decided on 1 percent precision and 99 percent reliability. This resulted in a sample size of 460 proxies, out of many thousands. Management was pleased with our plan. We carried it out and, as one would expect, found the proxy process to be completely reliable and to have integrity.

By the end of my third busy season, I was a bona fide statistical expert. I began serving all of the west coast offices, and by the time I became a manager, I had done work for offices throughout The Firm.

Discussion Questions

7–1 *Is an "up-or-out" policy sensible in managing a CPA firm in today's environment?*

7–2 *What is the turnover rate in public accounting in your community today, and how is it expected to change?*

7–3 *Have you ever participated in a formal employee evaluation before? If so, what were its strengths and weaknesses?*

7–4 *What are the advantages and disadvantages of large-company and small-company client assignments?*

7–5 *How adequately has your college experience prepared you to develop good recommendations for future client improvements, or beyond that, to work on formal consulting engagements?*

7–6 *Do you think having consulting engagements for audit clients is a potential threat to auditor objectivity and independence?*

8

People Problems

As time went on and I became a more experienced senior, I found that I enjoyed the challenge of auditing very much. I looked at an audit as a special type of problem. There was a "reality" that was the client's true financial condition and results of operations. There was also a "representation" of that reality—the client's financial statements. The audit problem was to discover enough objective evidence and apply enough valid reasoning about the reality to be able to demonstrate that it was properly portrayed by the representation.

I also found that I enjoyed working with others. I guess I am a reasonably gregarious person. I'm certainly not an introvert. Explaining things to staff and clients, pulling a plan together, and having it carried out to everyone's satisfaction gives me a great deal of satisfaction. Over my first few years with The Firm, I also developed a strong affection for the partners and other staff members in the Oakland office. There were, however, two notable exceptions.

Stan Wright was a manager while I was a senior. The significant thing about Stan is that he was, and probably still is, a real jerk. He was the kind of guy who would intimidate the staff who worked for him in an attempt to get the maximum effort out of each of them. He believed that you *could* get blood out of a turnip. Stan would make unrealistic commitments for completing work and then require the staff on the job to make good on those commitments by working an unreasonable amount of hours. Also, Stan would always take credit for the results.

Stan would also ask staff to do things that they shouldn't do. His favorite practice was to "suggest" that they must *always* complete their work within the budgeted number of hours. He taught that if it looked as if the staff were going to go over the budget in an audit area, they could simply fail to record the excess hours worked. Of course, this would sandbag anybody who succeeded Stan on one of his jobs because the prior year's recorded hours would understate the true magnitude of the job.

Stan started in the San Francisco office and, billed as a "comer," was transferred to Oakland when the office started to grow. But he virtually "ate up" the staff. Not only would Stan overwork the staff, he would brag about the number of hours that specific staff under his supervision worked. Stan was asked to leave The Firm shortly after the first and only time I worked for him. I don't look back on the events of that engagement fondly, but they were instructive experiences for me.

I worked for Stan as the senior on the Ardmore Castings audit. Ardmore was a company that did custom castings for machinery manufacturers. Ardmore was a calendar-year client, but it was not publicly held, so the work didn't have to be completed by the March 31 SEC deadline. Nonetheless, Ardmore wanted the audit done as soon as practicable, so it followed right after SEC work. In effect, by my being assigned to Ardmore, my busy season was extended a couple of months beyond my participation on the Rineholt audit.

I wasn't originally scheduled to work on Ardmore. Unfortunately, the previous senior decided to leave The Firm just before the work was to begin. This was the type of scheduling crisis that is not at all uncommon in public accounting, and it is normally resolved by trading people around until there is a fit. Of course, "the fit" almost always requires overtime to keep the clients happy.

I had a couple of problems with the assignment. First of all, my fall and winter had been particularly demanding. My statistical jobs were building up to the point where that aspect of my work was taking on a life of its own. This was very satisfying to me, and it was enhancing my reputation and progress in The Firm. But it was the kind of thing that couldn't be subjected to longer-range planning. In effect, the jobs were always an imposition on what I was doing and required me to scramble to get them done. The good news was that I always got my full billing rate for the work done. This was noteworthy because the office's average writedown on work done was about 25 percent of standard billing rates.

The second problem was that Libby was pregnant with our first child, Jon, and was expected to deliver toward the end of April, right in the middle of the Ardmore work. I had thought we were pretty clever, planning Jon's birth after the busy season. Oh well, Robbie Burns, the best-laid plans . . . I had always made a point of discussing my work with Libby. I wanted her to know what was going on, how I was doing, and what to expect in a profession that is less predictable than it seems on the surface. When I told her about the Ardmore assignment, I could tell she was disappointed that I would still be working long hours, but she was as supportive as possible.

"Well, is this a good assignment for you?" she asked.

"I think so. It will give me some more experience in heavier manufacturing, which is good. I don't know too much about Stan, but I hope he'll be good to work for. The partner is Bill Jepsen. I've worked for him a couple of times and he's a good guy, although he's tied up on some other things, so I expect Stan will basically be running the show."

"Good, then there's a number of positives for you. I don't think you have to worry about me. I'm feeling fine and you'll be only a phone call away. And besides, you know Mom will be hanging around here every chance she gets."

"You know, Libby, there's also a chance I could make fifth-year manager. It could be a big help if this job goes really well and I get a good evaluation from Stan, who hasn't evaluated me before."

"There you go, then. Just do a good job, and I'll make sure everything is under control around here."

As usual, my conversation with Libby had the effect of making me feel as if everything *were* under control. Of course, I had no idea at the time how wrong I was in my assessment of Stan and of how he might serve as the catalyst for my promotion.

The Ardmore job started out as I might have expected, but then things went downhill fast. There were three other staff members on the engagement besides me: Al Wentworth, Sarah Lockington, and Barney Keppel. Barney had come over from Rineholt with me. As senior, I was in charge of the fieldwork, including supervision of the other three staff. Stan had laid out a plan for the audit in general terms and had written a memo on how the audit program would be changed. It was my responsibility to make the changes. Stan had also put together a time budget showing what areas he wanted each of us to be responsible for. I had somewhat of a debate with Stan about the time budget. The budget showed a 10 percent reduction in the total staff time from the previous year. I told Stan that I thought that the estimate was overly optimistic, especially since all of us except Stan and Bill Jepsen were new to the job. Also, since the company had grown, it seemed to me that there would be at least some increase in the amount of work that had to be done. I also wanted to be able to use my own judgment about assigning specific tasks to the other staff. I felt it was my job to motivate and develop them, and I needed some discretion to do that well.

Stan at first seemed irritated by my statements. He then relaxed, gave me a stare, and delivered a very unpleasant message. "You haven't worked for me before, Jack, so I guess I had better go over my rules with you."

Rules? I thought. This was the first time any manager, or partner for that matter, had ever talked to me about his or her "rules."

"The first rule is that I'm running the job. I don't mind getting your input, but I'm the manager and I'll make the decisions. The second rule is that on my jobs, the budget is always an improvement over last year, and we *always* make the budget. Now, as long as you and the others understand the rules, there will be no problem. Everyone will get a good evaluation, and life will be fine. If you don't like the rules, and if you're not willing to live by them, it's your tail in the wringer, Jack, not mine."

I couldn't believe this guy. I was working for Adolf Hitler, and he was threatening to exterminate me if I didn't toe the line. But I figured the best thing to do at that point was to keep my mouth shut. Maybe his style was to catch others off guard. I couldn't believe he was actually that hard-nosed.

Stan continued. "I'll come by every day at six. If you and the staff are going to eat dinner, be sure to be finished by the time I get here. I'll get a brief report from each of you about what you've done during the day, and I'll check the time summary. Then, I'll review workpapers. You can do the work for my review notes the same night or wait until the next day, but I want all the points cleaned up by the time I get back."

Stan wasn't treating me like a senior at all but more like just another staff under his direct control. I could feel my stomach sink. This was awful. Nevertheless, I decided I would have to go along with him. Probably the best thing I could do was to try to please him and then dedicate myself to not working for him again.

The work went along according to plan. During the daytime when Stan was absent, I gave the other staff as much support as I could while still getting my tasks done. We were putting in about 60 hours a week and everyone was stressed out. I tried to make jokes and keep everyone's spirits up. To be honest, though, it was a hollow effort, because my morale was dropping pretty fast.

When I went home at night, I'd flop into bed and Libby would rub my back and try to cheer me up. My God, she was the one about to give birth to a baby, and I was the one getting all the tender loving care. I was really starting to resent the situation I was in, and my feelings toward Stan grew stronger and stronger each day.

Then on the Friday of our fourth week, when we were about two-thirds of the way through the field work, a real problem arose. Just after 5:00 P.M., I went into the men's room to wash up before we grabbed a quick bite and got ready to meet our maker, Stan. When I entered the men's room, I noticed that one of the stall doors was closed and I heard sobbing, then the sound of vomiting, coming from behind the door.

"Barney, is that you?" I called.

"Yeah, Jack. Please just leave me alone."

"Come on, Barney. Are you sick? Can I get you anything?"

"I'll be all right. Just give me a few moments."

After about five minutes, Barney Keppel came out of the stall. He looked terrible. His face was flushed, his tie was pulled down, he had tears on his face, and he was almost hyperventilating. I put my right arm around Barney's shoulders and braced him up with my left hand. I said as gently as I could, "What is it, Barney? You can tell me. I'll help you out."

"Oh, Jack," Barney's tears started again. "My life is falling apart. I'm so tired I can't see straight, and my wife told me this morning that I've got to spend more time at home or she'll divorce me. I wake up every morning and have the dry heaves. I don't know what to do."

I'd never seen a person have a breakdown before. "Come on, Barney. Wash your face, fix your tie, and comb your hair. Then I'm going to drive you home. Your car will be okay here tonight. I'm the senior on this job, and it's my decision that we can complete it just fine with you working 40 hours a week. We'll tell your wife—June, right?—that your busy season's over and you can get things back on track. The other thing is that tomorrow's Saturday. Come pick up your car, but take the day to rest up. And, Barney, I want you to see a doctor as soon as possible. Tomorrow morning if you can. I'm afraid you've let yourself run down. I haven't lost anybody on any of my jobs yet, and I won't let you be the first. Okay?"

Barney looked better, but still apprehensive. "What about Stan, Jack? He's not going to like this one bit. He may not go for it."

"He'll go for it because he won't have a choice. If he gives you any ultimatums, I guarantee you he'll have to get a new senior for the job. He can't take that chance. And as far as your evaluation goes, I'm your immediate supervisor, so mine will lay everything out the way it is. Don't worry about this stuff, Barney. You've got higher priorities right now."

I took Barney home and then went home myself. I told Libby what had happened and that I did what I thought was right, but I had probably killed off any chance of receiving a good evaluation from Stan and an early promotion.

At about 7:00 P.M. the phone rang; it was Stan. "Just what in hell do you think you're doing, Butler? I don't mind if you don't work late on Fridays, but I expect you to be here for our meeting, and where's Keppel?" It was obvious that Al and Sarah had acted dumb.

I told Stan that Barney had become ill, that in my opinion he needed medical help and more rest than he was getting, and that I had committed to him a 40-hour workweek for the rest of the audit.

Stan blew his stack. "You committed, *you* committed? Just who the hell do you think you are? Here's a commitment to you, Jack: I commit to have you out the door of this firm just as soon as this audit is over. If I can't do that, then I'll make damn sure you become The Firm's oldest living senior."

I had had it. "You do what you think you have to do, Stan. But I did what I believed was the proper thing to do in the circumstances tonight, and I'd do it again without thinking twice. I'll get your job finished for you on time and within budget. And then I'll tell Jed that if I'm ever asked to work for you again, I'll quit. You're a real piece of work, Stan. Thank God there aren't any others around like you."

We wrapped up the Ardmore audit on time. I was fortunate that the technical audit was routine—no big surprises, no big problems. Barney came back to life and told me he had the start of an ulcer, but that it was being treated successfully. Also, he and his wife had made amends.

The big surprise came a month after the engagement was completed. Bill Jepsen called me into his office and told me he had heard what had happened on the Ardmore job with Barney and Stan. He apologized for not being around more and complimented me on the way I handled things. He said that Stan was leaving The Firm. He showed me Stan's evaluation of me, which Stan had never discussed with me as he was supposed to. Bill also showed me a memo that he had written overriding Stan's evaluation. In his memo, Bill stated that he believed I showed mature judgment and sound technical skills, and that I was ready for promotion to manager that year. And, in fact, it came to pass.

The second "people" problem I had that year involved one of my construction company clients. A number of my off-season clients were construction companies. This was an area of industry concentration for the Oakland office. Most construction companies were privately held, but they needed an audit for financing and bonding purposes. By the time I was a senior, I considered myself to have a fair amount of construction expertise. I enjoyed my construction clients. The companies were owned and managed by people who built things—houses, buildings, bridges, and roads. They were not exactly rough-and-tumble, but they were people who spent a lot of their time out-of-doors and knew how to get things done. They were generally considerate of others and possessed integrity as human beings and as businesspeople. I liked the type.

C&L Construction was a client that specialized in heavy construction. It had projects not only in northern and southern California but also in Oregon, Nevada, and Arizona. Most of its jobs were completed in a matter of months, but some took more than a year. At any one time, it had ten to fifteen jobs in process.

Toward the end of my third year with The Firm, I was assigned to senior the audit of C&L. The partner on the job was Roy Shantz, partner in charge of the tax department. Roy had been a friend of Frank Lethridge, the company's owner, for many years. Roy oversaw his tax work, and he convinced The Bear that he should also be the audit partner, for the sake of good client relations. It seemed like a low-risk audit situation, so Barnes agreed. There had been a manager assigned to the job, but he'd left The Firm just before the work began. No other managers were available, so Roy decided to rely more directly on me as the senior and to use two staff for the field work instead of just one. I was a glutton for responsibility, so the plan was fine with me.

The main task in auditing a construction company is evaluating the probable outcome of the projects that are in process at the end of the fiscal year. Income is generally recognized using the percentage-of-completion method. This requires estimating costs to complete the projects as well as their ultimate profit or loss. For projects that will result in a profit, the company will recognize a proportionate share of the project's profit through year end. For projects that will result in a loss, however, the entire estimated loss must be recognized. This is usually done by debiting a project loss account on the income statement and crediting a provision for project loss account on the liability side of the balance sheet.

Generally, the approach to this aspect of the audit is to review project bid worksheets, to audit costs to date, to discuss the progress on projects with project engineers, to physically inspect projects, and to talk to management about their expectations for each project. I completed all of these steps for C&L except for discussing the projects with Frank Lethridge. The reason I did not do that was that I concluded that there was a high probability that several of the projects would result in a loss. I contacted Roy Shantz about this problem and he said he would talk to Lethridge himself.

Shantz came over to C&L's offices when we had completed everything on the audit except for the final discussion of projects in process. I assumed that Shantz would include me in his meeting with Lethridge, but after I went over the project workpapers with him, he told me that he wanted to talk to Lethridge alone. This seemed very strange to me, but mine wasn't to question why; he was the engagement partner. Shantz met with Lethridge for about two hours. When he came out of the meeting, he told me, "These jobs will all produce a profit, Jack. Here are the numbers I want you to enter into the project estimate worksheet." He handed me a piece of paper with his notes on it. "Throw this away after you transfer the numbers. I'll write a memo on my meeting with Frank and add it to the workpapers when I do my final review and sign-off."

The next morning in our office, I entered the job profit estimates and wrapped up the workpapers. As I did these tasks, I felt very uneasy about the way Shantz had handled this aspect of the audit, and about my role in it. I thought my preliminary judgments were good, and I resented not being allowed to discuss them with Shantz and Lethridge, at least to see where I might be off base. But I was late starting my next job, and I realize now that I used that as an excuse to just accept Shantz's authority and judgment in the circumstances. I left the workpapers with Shantz's secretary and went on to my next assignment. I never heard anything further from Shantz, so I assumed he was satisfied with the job we had done after his workpaper review. I subsequently heard that C&L had been sold to a large construction firm in Texas and that we wouldn't be doing any work for it again.

About 18 months after we completed that last C&L audit, Roy Shantz called me into his office and introduced me to Marvin Rester and Mary Ann Smith. Marvin and Mary Ann were attorneys representing Frank Lethridge as a defendant in a lawsuit brought by the company that had purchased C&L from him. More precisely, they represented Frank's estate, since he had died of heart failure in the interim. It seems that the Texas construction company had experienced significant losses on several of the projects it acquired from C&L. In the purchase agreement for the sale, Lethridge had guaranteed that recorded liabilities were not understated. The purchasing company was suing under breach of contract on the theory that since the provision for future contract losses was a credit on the liability side of the balance sheet, it was a liability, and since there were unrecorded losses, it was an understated liability for which Lethridge was responsible. The Firm was not named in the suit; however, Shantz and I would be called as witnesses in Lethridge's defense. This would require giving deposition testimony to the plaintiff's attorneys and then testifying in court. At that stage in my career, I had not given a deposition or testified in court, but I had heard a dozen horror stories about people who had. I was pretty nervous about the whole thing. Marvin and Mary Ann coached me on the process and tried to alleviate my fears by telling me to give brief, forthright answers and to be honest if I didn't know something or couldn't recall.

The plaintiff's attorney who took my deposition seemed like a nice enough guy. He didn't try to intimidate me or anything like that. Basically, he was just trying to gather as much information as possible about the accounting that was done. Throughout the deposition, Marvin was at my side to advise me on the deposition procedure and to enter objections where he thought the questioning departed from the procedural rules.

The questions revolved around two issues. The first was whether the provision for probable future losses on contracts in progress was, in fact, a liability. I said it was not in the conventional sense where the company owes payment to an outside party as the result of a transaction entered into with that party; rather, it was a credit that arises under generally accepted accounting principles as a result of matching losses to the period in which they applied. We talked around this issue for a couple of hours. As we did, I visualized myself trying to explain this level of accounting technology to a jury and couldn't imagine twelve ordinary people being able to understand it.

The second issue was the amount of the provision in light of the fact that profits were forecast on several jobs that eventually experienced a loss. The plaintiff's attorney laid the relevant workpapers out in front of me and went over each of them in complete detail. He asked where each comment, tick mark, and number had come from and what they meant. I found that I had a hard time recalling all these details, even though only 18 months had passed.

The big question, of course, was, "How did you satisfy yourself that these final job forecasts were reasonable?" I responded that they were based on a conference and review of underlying project data with Frank Lethridge. The attorney asked who handled the conference and where it was documented. I fumbled through the workpapers looking for Shantz's memo, which wasn't to be found. All I could find was our standard partner sign-off form indicating that in Roy's opinion, the financial statements complied with GAAP and our audit had been done in accordance with GAAS. The best I could do was to say that my recollection was that Mr. Shantz had conducted the conference and that he was satisfied.

Two weeks later, Marvin called and asked me to meet with him. After we exchanged pleasantries, Marvin told me that he was concerned about an apparent contradiction between my deposition testimony and Shantz's. He asked me to read a section of Shantz's. When the plaintiff's attorney asked Shantz about the final conference concerning project profit forecasts, he responded that he could not recall ever having had such a conference and that I must have had it. He said that in signing off on the audit, he did not believe he had to conduct any procedures. His testimony was: "I had complete confidence in Jack Butler and signed off after only doing a workpaper review."

Needless to say, I was upset by this. It was clear to me that Shantz had lied under oath to protect himself, and that if anything negative came out of this lawsuit, I would end up looking like the bad guy. Fortunately, Lethridge's estate and the buyer settled the suit. Although legitimate questions existed concerning the accounting issues, Lethridge did have a good case that the jobs lost money because the Texas company mismanaged them after they left C&L's hands. Although I never had to testify in court, for a long time afterward I pondered the situation I had found myself in. What should I have done differently?

Discussion Questions

8–1 What alternatives did Jack have to deciding to put up with Stan's attitude and treatment as his supervisor?

8–2 What should a staff person do if he or she is asked to do something he or she considers to be unethical?

8–3 What responsibility does a supervisor have to a subordinate who is having personal problems?

8–4 How important are staff evaluations, and why?

8–5 What elements would an ideal personnel evaluation system contain?

8–6 Is it appropriate for a tax or consulting partner to have primary responsibility for an audit engagement?

8–7 To what extent should a staff person question the judgment or instructions of a partner?

8–8 What steps can a staff person take when he or she disagrees with the judgments made by superiors on an audit engagement?

8–9 How likely is it that a professional auditor will be involved in a litigation situation during his or her career, and what do you think the experience is like?

8–10 Was Shantz's behavior in connection with the C&L audit and the subsequent litigation unethical, and, if so, how?

8–11 What should Jack have done differently on the C&L audit?

9
People Solutions

lthough my experiences with Stan Wright and Roy Shantz were salient and disconcerting, they were far outnumbered by good experiences. Several of the good ones involved Quentin Barnes and the way he backed me up. One I will never forget happened in the fall of my fourth year. We had a client called California Holdings, Inc., a holding company whose main asset was a savings and loan association in Stockton, California. The holding company had raised capital through the sale of stock, with the controlling block owned by the company's CEO, George Pearson. The holding company was headquartered in Oakland because Pearson lived in the adjacent community of Piedmont. The Bear was the partner on the job because he had known Pearson over the years. The savings and loan subsidiary was audited by our Sacramento office, and we consolidated it with the holding company and issued our opinion on the consolidated financial statements in Oakland. Because the amount of work done in Oakland was relatively minor, there was no manager on the job. As senior, I reported directly to Barnes.

Pearson was an interesting case. Apparently, he had had his ups and downs over the years, becoming a millionaire and then losing his fortune several times. He hoped to use California Holdings as a vehicle to move into various financial services, and he hoped to be able to acquire other companies using stock. He knew he would dilute his interest, but he thought that he could make acquisitions without giving up overall control. And, of course, the real problem was that he was short of cash and couldn't do it any other way.

Pearson had one personal habit that amazed me: He owned a limousine and employed a full-time chauffeur. He loved to schedule a meeting in his office and send his chauffeur to pick up his guest. This might not seem so strange in New York, but in Oakland? Pearson had found a way to distinguish himself; how people might react to it was another matter. The Bear told me that Pearson had maintained his car and chauffeur throughout all of his ups and downs. Apparently, his priorities were such that his car and chauffeur would be the last things that he would sacrifice. He seemed like a nice enough guy, even if a little strange. Perhaps *affected* would be a better word to describe him.

California Holdings had a small accounting staff and relied on us actually to put the statements together, including drafting the footnotes. This is the usual practice with all but our largest clients. The audited financial statements of the savings and loan, which were required for regulatory purposes, were completed in Sacramento. The audited financial statements of the consolidated holding company, which were required because there were outside stockholders, were done by me in Oakland.

I started the holding company audit about a week before we expected the savings and loan report to be completed. Most of the work involved verifying assets and debt. In doing this, I found that some new debt had been acquired and transferred to the savings and loan in the form of a capital contribution. Things had not been going well for the association, and additional capital was needed to meet federal capital requirements. The bank that made the loan required that the physical assets owned by the holding company, which included several commercial buildings, be put forth as collateral for the debt. There was also a working capital loan that was secured by some notes receivable held by the holding company. When I drafted the financial statements, I disclosed these collateral arrangements in a footnote and referenced the note next to each asset that served as collateral.

After the audit work was completed, and the financial statements and our report were drafted and typed, I took them into Pearson's office for his review and approval. He skipped over our report and focused on the balance sheet. He balked and looked up at me. "What are these references next to the assets about the debt?"

"Those are standard references that show that the assets are subject to collateral agreements," I replied.

"I don't want those there. Take 'em out."

"I can't do that, Mr. Pearson. They have to be there for the financial statements to meet the rules."

Pearson just looked at me. His lips and jaw muscles began to tighten and he began to tremble slightly. Then he did something that I couldn't believe. He picked up his phone and said to his secretary, "Get me Quentin Barnes, right now!"

I started to explain the situation further, but Pearson held up his hand and said, "I don't want to hear it." So we just sat and stared at each other until the phone rang.

"Quentin, this is George Pearson. You've got a guy over here named Jack Butler. I am sending him back to your office as soon as I hang up the phone. I don't ever want to see him here again, and I suggest that you consider firing him." He paused, "That's right." And he handed me the phone.

"Hello," I said.

"Jack, it's me," said The Bear at the other end. "Listen to me, Jack, don't lose your cool here. I know you haven't done anything wrong. Just calmly put down the phone, say a polite good-bye to the idiot across the desk from you, and come on back over to the office. And be sure to bring all of our papers with you. Okay, Jack?"

"Okay," I replied, and followed his instructions.

Back in the office, Bear gave me a malicious grin. "I figured old Pearson was about ready to flip," he said. "He's under a lot of pressure from his outside stockholders to pull a rabbit out of a hat, and with the thrift industry in the doldrums, I don't think he can do it. Now, tell me word for word exactly what happened."

I went through the events with The Bear, showing him the workpapers, the draft report, and my list of what was left to be done on the engagement. Bear agreed with my assessment and placed a call to Pearson.

"George, it's Quentin. Have you settled down yet? Good. Now here's the deal, George. My guy Butler has done a first-class job on your audit. He's absolutely right about the collateral disclosures. There is no way I'll sign the audit report without them. I don't know what's bothering you, George, but you jumped all over Jack for no good reason. I think you owe both of us an apology. All right, George, here he is."

Bear handed me the phone. "Jack, I'm sorry, I apologize," Pearson said. "I knew the damn financial statements weren't going to look as good as I wanted them to, and I just lost my head and took it out on you."

"I appreciate your situation, Mr. Pearson. I accept your apology."

I handed the phone back to The Bear. "Okay, George, thank you. To-morrow at 12:15 will be fine." Bear looked at me and grinned. "He's sending his driver to get us at 12:15 tomorrow to take us to his club for lunch."

Another event that sticks out in my memory happened during July of my fourth year. Things were slow for a couple of weeks, and I found myself sitting in the staff room having coffee with Bobby Hirada. Bobby had started with The Firm in the Oakland office the year after I did. He had earned a degree from an Ivy League business school. Bobby was extremely sharp and was doing very well with The Firm.

As we talked, we found ourselves basically in a "bitch" session, complaining about things in the office that bothered us. Then a thought occurred to me. "You know, Bobby, I hate someone who complains but isn't willing to do anything about the situation. But that's what you and I are doing now."

"I guess you're right. So what do you suggest we do?"

"I think we ought to do the same thing for the office that we do for our clients. We ought to write The Bear a management letter. We could spell out all the little things that bother us, and then give him suggestions on what we believe should be done."

"That's a good idea, but don't you think he'll just consider us a couple of smart-asses and file the letter in his wastebasket?"

"Sure, that's a possibility, but if we're really thoughtful and constructive, he might like it. He's a good guy, Bobby; even if he ignores our advice, I think he'll respect what we're trying to do."

So we put our heads together and wrote the letter. It took us about a week. The letter was twelve pages long, detailing nineteen specific problem areas and explaining our recommendations. The letter included a wide assortment of items, from dealing with conflicts over shared office space, to having a better method of getting messages, to the idea of staff's being privy to office financial and operating results. I felt that the way we presented our letter to Barnes was very important. When we were ready, I called Madeline and made an appointment to see him. At the appointed time, Bobby and I went to his office and told him, as earnestly as we could, what our idea was and what we had done. We emphasized that we were not trying to be critical, but that we were trying to be helpful. We also said that if he decided not to accept the letter, we would understand.

Bear listened and then responded, "I'm not offended by this, fellows. I'll be happy to read what you have to say. I won't promise anything, but I certainly will give your letter my attention and thought." He thanked us and sent us on our way.

About six weeks later, The Bear called a staff meeting. He did this about four or five times a year to bring everyone up to date on things or to discuss some particular problem. He started this staff meeting with a statement. "The reason I called this meeting is to acknowledge Jack Butler and Bobby Hirada for their initiative and positive attitude about being employees of this firm." He then went on actually to review our letter with the entire office. He stated that he had grouped the problems we cited and had assigned them to subgroups of people in the office to study. He said he wanted the subgroups to consider the seriousness of our concerns and to consider possible solutions. Our recommendations would become part of that process. Madeline had made up assignment packets for everyone, and we were to meet on the third Friday of each month for the rest of the year to discuss each subgroup's findings and to implement improvements.

Bobby and I were thrilled. We never expected anything like this. Others in the office congratulated us on our initiative and on our ideas. We got a lot of, "You know, this problem has been bothering me ever since I came here. Now something might actually be done about it. I'm sure glad you guys pointed it out in your letter."

The subgroup to which I was assigned examined the question of how much information should be shared with the staff. Up to that point in time, The Firm had a very patriarchal view of not letting the staff in on the results of operations and related financial matters. Managers got to see billing analyses for individual clients and we each knew what our utilization was, but that was about it. I expected that things were that way out of fear of the unknown more than anything else. The partners probably felt that bad news might cause panic among the staff with premature departures and that good news might cause the staff to develop unrealistic expectations and to make inappropriate demands.

As our subgroup discussed the pros and cons of sharing more information with the staff, we recognized those concerns. We also heard the argument that the staff members should be concentrating on their professional responsibilities and that giving the staff members more information might serve to distract them from that necessary focus. However, there were several compelling arguments in favor of more information. First was the idea that public accounting is *both* a profession and a business; if The Firm wants the staff members to develop into effective partners, it should give them responsibility for the business side as well as the professional side of the practice. Developing as businesspersons implies providing the staff with appropriate information for that purpose. Another equally pragmatic argument was that the staff members, who are well-educated and experienced professionals, in fact have skills that could help solve Firm business problems—why not take advantage of those skills?

There were also several behavioral arguments. Providing more information would demonstrate a sense of openness and confidence in the staff members and would give them a stronger feeling of connection with the firm. Furthermore, providing valid information would help prevent misinformation and rumors. And involving staff members with information could serve as an incentive for them to do a better job in gathering or providing information when they are asked to do so.

Our subgroup recommended that the office develop a monthly report to staff that would contain key financial information and accompanying operating statistics. The report should be set up in a way that would clearly state the relationship between staff actions and results. The report should be one copy, marked confidential, and kept in a central location under someone's specific control, so that staff members could come and review it as they had time.

Our proposal and the proposals from the other subgroups were received and discussed at the subsequent staff meetings, which The Bear came to call "Improvement Meetings." They resulted in a number of positive changes. In some cases, the subgroups decided that a problem wasn't significant enough to call for changes, although communication about it was an obvious benefit. In some cases, such as with the issue of the sharing of information, we had to get clearance from the national office before we could modify Firm policies to meet our needs. The two greatest benefits, I believe, were starting everyone down the path of looking for ways to make things better and witnessing The Bear's willingness to underwrite the effort.

The overriding thing that The Bear did to be supportive was simply to create the honest belief that anyone in the office could talk to him without being afraid. When I say "simply," I don't intend to imply that it was easy to do. I expect it was very difficult. Nonetheless, The Bear developed this belief and maintained it—for example, by allowing people to call him by his nickname, Bear. The principle that he followed was trust. In other words, if a person earned Barnes's trust, then that person could be sure that Barnes would be honest with him or her, listen to what he or she had to say, take it at face value, and try to help the person along the right path. At the same time, there were instances where someone lied to Barnes or took advantage of The Firm, and Barnes dealt decisively with that person in some other way.

I can recall a couple of those instances clearly. One involved Darcy Hancock, a very assertive woman who came to work in the Oakland office the year after I did. During orientation, The Bear always emphasized the importance of maintaining absolute client confidentiality. Of course, confidentiality is a principle of auditing and is included as a specific item in the *Rules of Conduct*. But Darcy liked to blow her own horn, a lot. Whenever she did something she was proud of, she would talk about it *ad nauseam* with everyone she met. That went for personal things like seeing a movie, getting a new car, or going on a vacation. Unfortunately, it went for business matters as well.

Darcy's second year with The Firm was an election year. As a member of the Young Republicans, she attended a posh fund-raising dinner that was being held for the Republican senatorial candidate at the Mark Hopkins Hotel in San Francisco. While she was standing with a group at the pre-dinner cocktail party, Darcy started talking about the interesting work she was doing. The work involved developing some pre-merger analyses for her client. She proceeded to tell her audience about a possible merger that had not yet been announced to the public. Unbeknownst to Darcy, a member of the board of directors of the client company was talking to someone standing just behind her. He heard her remarks, found out who she was, and called The Bear at home the next morning.

Nobody except Darcy and Barnes knows for sure what he said to her, but it is known that The Bear called Darcy at her apartment that Saturday morning and told her to meet him in the office at once. Darcy met with The Bear, left his office, cleared out her desk, and never entered the Oakland office of The Firm again. The last I heard, she had gone back to graduate school and had gotten a job with a large bank.

The second instance of Barnes's handling of a personnel problem involved Kenneth Spruance. Kenneth was from a well-to-do Marin County family. He had gone to prep school and to a private college. He dressed well, had a new car, and lived in a much nicer apartment than most of us. Kenneth could afford all this because he had inherited some family money. He didn't use his wealth to gain any particular advantage—it just showed through his natural ways. One of those ways was Kenneth's love of the chase. He had enough money to go out every night if he wished, and he generally did. Although he was young and strong, he was also having a difficult time making it to jobs on time and working efficiently before 10 o'clock in the morning.

When The Bear became aware of Kenneth's behavior, he called him in for a heart-to-heart. He didn't threaten or even scold Kenneth, he just reasoned with him in terms of what Kenneth's goals were and what The Firm required of its staff. Kenneth was contrite, thanked The Bear for his advice, and made a commitment to tone down his social life to the point that it didn't interfere with his job responsibilities. For the next several months, Kenneth was at work on time, alert and productive.

But then the other aspect of his social habits got the best of him. He was working at Rineholt in the engineering division. The secretary to the controller was a very attractive redhead named Betsy Martindale. All of the male staff members who worked on the Rineholt audit knew and admired Betsy, but only one of them was dumb enough to make a move on her—that's right, it was Kenneth. Not only did Kenneth make a move, he advertised it by having two dozen long-stemmed roses delivered to Betsy at her desk in the Rineholt building. Betsy was putting the roses in water when two people approached her at the same time—Kenneth from the audit work area and her boss from inside his office. They met head on, so to speak, and Betsy smiled at Kenneth, then turned to her boss and said, "Mr. Graves, look at the beautiful flowers Kenneth sent me."

I suppose it would be all right for Kenneth to date someone who works for Rineholt if he weren't involved on the job, but to date the secretary of the controller was not only against Firm policy and office practice, it showed incredibly bad judgment on Kenneth's part. The Bear talked to him about the call he got from Graves expressing his objection to Kenneth and Betsy's having a relationship. But he didn't crucify him as some might expect. The fact was that Bear really liked Kenneth, and they decided between them that public accounting was probably too constraining to keep Kenneth happy. Kenneth left shortly thereafter. Now whenever The Bear talks about Kenneth, he always says that Kenneth's problem was that he considered sex more important than accounting. Then he laughs and adds that if it isn't, we're all in trouble.

My own experience in talking to The Bear about a difficult subject came in the fall of my fourth year. I was working at Rineholt on a Friday morning when Bob Arosco, the CFO of Cement, asked me if I would have a chat with him. We went into his office, and I became apprehensive when he closed the door and asked his secretary to hold all of his calls. But he was relaxed and smiling, so I figured it wasn't a "problem meeting."

Bob came right to the point. "Jack, I'm looking for a new controller for Gypsum, and I'd like you to consider yourself a candidate for the job." This caught me by surprise in one sense but not in another. I knew that Gypsum's controller was retiring, but I had no idea that Arosco was considering me. I said I was flattered and that I would certainly have an open mind about the opportunity.

The terms that Arosco outlined were very attractive. The job would pay about $1,000 more a month than I was currently making, there would be five weeks' vacation instead of the three weeks I currently enjoyed, and the fringe package included a profit-sharing plan. He also defined a career path of other, more responsible controllerships that could eventually lead to a CFO position, providing I earned it. Also, it was a way I could move into industry without having to move from Montclair.

After some discussion, I thanked Arosco once more and told him I would give it some thought over the weekend and tell him on Monday morning whether I wanted to be a candidate. I then called Madeline and asked if The Bear could possibly see me before he went home that evening. After a short wait, Madeline told me to come in at 4:00 P.M.

I told The Bear the general terms of Arosco's offer. I told him that this was the first "real" offer I had received and that I would appreciate any advice he could give me. Bear told me that receiving offers was something that I would continue to experience as long as I worked in public accounting and did a good job. He said that at the least, I should look at it as a positive indicator that my career was moving along the way it should. Then he said, "You know, Jack, when you were in college, you had a perception about public accounting and a perception about industry. Now you've worked on audits for almost four years, so you're more grounded in experience and reality. Do you want to go into industry?"

"I'm not sure," I replied. "When I left graduate school, my long-range plan was to eventually go into industry, to become a CFO. That's why I got an MBA instead of an MPrA degree. I figured public accounting would give me a great path."

"And it has, hasn't it?" Bear added. "You just got an offer that would lead in that direction. Don't be deceived by Arosco's proposal. I can tell you for sure that he never would have approached you unless you were his number-one candidate.

"Let me ask it this way, do you want to stay in public accounting?"

"I had always thought I'd at least want to be a manager," I said. "I figured that would make me a candidate for a better set of corporate positions than if I left as a senior."

"I think that's true. My observation has been that as a general rule, the longer you wait to leave, the better a position you will leave for. But what I'm really interested in, Jack, is do you *like* public accounting?"

"That goes without saying. I like auditing, I like the variety, I've liked the tax work I've done, I think my clients are super, my statistical stuff is going well, the office is a great place to work. I really have no complaints, except perhaps the grind toward the end of the busy season."

"What do you think you would like and dislike about the job at Gypsum?"

"Well, the money and the fringes are certainly attractive. And I think I'd like being part of building a larger organization. Although the cement industry isn't growing, Rineholt overall is doing well. I think the long-term career path is pretty good.

"As for what I might not like, I suppose it's going to the same place and seeing the same faces every day. Dealing with administrative problems isn't something I'm crazy about. And I'd miss being part of a large peer group."

"If you had decided to go into industry and you could pick any company to work for that you wanted, would it be Rineholt Cement?"

"Probably not. I'd probably chose a little faster-moving, entrepreneurial situation."

"Jack, this is your decision, and however you make it, you'll have my blessing and all the help you need. But in making it, I think you should realize that you're doing very well here. Arosco may have big plans for you, but we have plans for you too. If I understand you correctly, you didn't come into public accounting thinking you might become a partner someday, but that is an option, and you should think about it as you make this decision."

"You're not offering me a partnership now, are you, Bear?" I joked.

"You know me better than that, Jack. That's something I couldn't do even if I thought you were ready. No, what I'm telling you is that you're on track. People like you, you've done an excellent job on engagements, you show good judgment, and you're willing to learn and to grow. When I compare you with people who have made partner, I see you operating on the same level as they did at the same stage in their careers."

At that point, it seemed as if we both had said what we wanted to say. I thanked The Bear for his advice and for taking the time to see me. I told him that I would know what I would do by the end of the weekend, and that I would call him Monday morning to let him know.

I spoke to Libby about the offer and my talk with The Bear and asked her to help me make the decision. I told her that anything like this was *our* decision, not *my* decision. She laughed. "Come on, Jack, you know you've already decided what you're going to do. I could tell when you talked about your meeting with Quentin. You're not ready to leave The Firm yet, are you?"

"It's hard to turn down another $1,000 a month, Lib."

"No it's not. What would be hard would be for you to stop going to work every day hardly able to hold yourself down at the breakfast table because you want to get going so badly."

"Am I really like that?"

"I'll videotape you and you can see for yourself. Now go call Quentin and give him the good news. You don't want the poor man to worry the whole weekend that he might lose his best staff man."

My experiences with Quentin Barnes, both the direct and the indirect ones, taught me that although organizations have names and legal statuses, they are basically a collection of people. A person doesn't really work for the organization; he or she works for those people. One's true success as an employee should be measured in terms of the nature of his or her relationships with the others in the organization. I felt that I had developed a rich relationship with The Bear, open and based on mutual respect and trust—things that are hard to walk away from.

Discussion Questions

9–1 *How might one deal with a "difficult" client, both in terms of restraining one's own emotions and in communicating with the client in difficult circumstances?*

9–2 *What should people do when they find that there are things about the organization they work for that really bother them?*

9–3 *What should people do when they realize that their personal goals seem to be in conflict with those of the organization?*

9–4 *In what ways is a public accounting practice a business as well as a professional organization, and what conflicts does this give rise to?*

9–5 *Was Barnes's treatment of Darcy Hancock appropriate and fair?*

9–6 *Was Barnes's handling of Kenneth Spruance appropriate and fair?*

9–7 *If one is to leave public accounting to go into industry, when is the best time to initiate such a move?*

9–8 *What are likely reasons to leave public accounting? What are likely reasons to stay?*

10

Thinking Like a Partner

Receiving my promotion to manager after four instead of five years was a real boost to my view of myself as a member of The Firm and of the public accounting profession. I continued to think about The Bear's words of advice and encouragement, and I began to take the idea of staying with The Firm and becoming a partner more seriously. I received notice of my promotion during my annual evaluation, which was conducted that year by Bill Jepsen. Bill congratulated me, told me what my salary increase would be, and went over my strengths and weaknesses. This year, however, he conducted the review in a different context.

"Jack, now that you're a manager, you've got to start thinking like a partner. I know you've already started to do that, because of the letter you and Bobby wrote. That was a very mature thing to do. But now I'd like you to visualize what attributes and skills a partner would have and to compare yourself to that. Then you can develop a plan to get from where you are to where you should be. In fact, I'd like you to do it in writing and discuss your plan with me two weeks from today, same time, here in my office."

I gave Bill's request most of my attention for the next two weeks. It seemed to me that he had affirmed Bear's message about my potential, and I thought that the exercise he was having me go through was a chance to challenge my own sense of desire about being a partner. When I considered what attributes a partner should have, I divided them into three general groups: technical skills, practice skills, and behavioral skills. The technical skills included an understanding of GAAS and GAAP, an ability to recognize clients' business problems and to come up with creative solutions, an in-depth understanding of at least one primary industry, and a reasonable ability to keep up with computer technology. The practice skills I identified were good administrative skills, good billing and collection practices, and an ability to bring in new business. Finally, the behavioral skills I listed included an ability to motivate staff under sometimes difficult working conditions and strong communications skills—listening, speaking, and writing.

When I compared this list with my own assessment, as well as Bill's assessment, of my personal strengths and weaknesses, I focused my plan for the future on two things: becoming a good business developer and improving my expertise in the construction industry. I met with Bill and presented him with what I had done. His reaction was positive. He stated that I would have to demonstrate an ability to bring in business in order to be successful in the long run. He emphasized that industry expertise was one of the strategies I could follow to develop business. As we talked about this, I expressed some reluctance to becoming too much of an industry expert.

"Why is that?" Bill asked.

"Well, a couple of reasons. If I spend all my time on construction companies, I'll have to give up a lot, particularly my position on the Rineholt audit."

"I think you're right about that. It's important to have a strong client base, and you've got a good start with Rineholt. I certainly couldn't advise you to give that up."

"And then there's the problem that I'd lose my flexibility in general. I don't want to become known as being so specialized that people may think I can't do anything else. You know, Bill, I like doing a number of different things. Variety is one of the reasons that this job is fun."

"Okay," said Bill. "I think what you've said makes sense. So then the plan is you'll continue to emphasize construction, but not to the exclusion of Rineholt and some other things. And, you'll really begin to bear down in your business development activities. Anything else?"

I replied, "Well, I had thought about one other possibility that I wanted to discuss with you."

"What's that?"

"I'm not saying I want to do this, but what about a 2-year stint in the national office? It would be a way to improve my technical skills, and it would be interesting to find out about The Firm in a more global sense. Of course, I realize that that would involve moving and disrupting my progress here."

"It's not a bad strategy, Jack. A lot of people do that and advance because of it. But you might want to consider that the chances of coming back to the Oakland office and moving back into Rineholt might be problematical. Also it's difficult to develop your business development skills in the national office. But if you think you might really want to do it, I'll be happy to initiate some movement on the idea for you."

At that, I began to wish I hadn't said anything about the idea. I was sure Libby and I would enjoy two years away, but I was also sure we would be less happy spending the rest of our working lives away from Oakland. I told Bill that on second thought, we ought not to consider it further.

"Okay. Do you think you should do anything else?"

"I don't think so, Bill. Don't you think the construction industry and business development will give me plenty to do during the next year or two, in addition to all the normal stuff?"

"Yes, but realistically, Jack, I think The Firm has higher expectations of its partners and managers than what may always seem reasonable. I was thinking that you would make a great office training director next year. How would you like that?"

I had always liked training. I had helped work up and put on several local office training sessions over the years and had enjoyed the experience. I was flattered by Bill's suggestion, and my immediate reaction was to welcome the opportunity. It also occurred to me that I had an additional opportunity here.

"I'll tell you what, Bill, I'll make a deal with you."

Bill got a quizzical look that turned suspecting after a moment. "What deal, Jack?"

"I'll gladly be the training director next year if you'll pull whatever strings you have to for me to be a group leader at Group I School next summer."

"Deal accepted," Bill smiled. "I thought you were going to ask for more money—that *would* have been a problem."

The other person who made fifth-year manager from my class in the Oakland office was Don Parnell. This delighted me because Don and I were such good friends. I was a little worried that if I were the only person in my group to receive early promotion, it would somehow drive a wedge between me and the rest. I enjoyed my association with the group and I wanted to sustain it as long as I could. By the time of my promotion, though, two of the six others who joined The Firm with me had already left to take positions elsewhere.

Like me, Don had been assigned to the Rineholt audit when we joined The Firm. He was assigned to the Engineering division, which did major construction all over the world—bridges, dams, that sort of thing. Don was a very efficient auditor, but more important, he had tremendous technical skills. It didn't take long before Don gained a reputation as *the* person in the office to go to if one didn't understand a particular accounting pronouncement. Don was also a computer whiz and was always helping people in that area. One of Don's strengths, or perhaps weaknesses, was that he would never say "no" when he was asked for help. This, along with his technical skills, endeared him to everyone in the office.

In Don's fourth year, he did something that kept The Firm out of a very serious problem. Rineholt was building a dam in Brazil. It was a major reclamation project in that country and had received a great deal of press. It was a huge, multi-million-dollar project for Rineholt. Rineholt had "bid it close" as part of a strategy to enhance its reputation in South America, hoping to get more profitable work in the future.

Don and the engagement manager traveled to Brazil to inspect the job, test job accounting records, and discuss the status of the project with the project manager and engineers. Things went pretty much as planned, but when Don examined cost records for the powerhouse portion of the project, he noticed that twice as much cost had been incurred for drilling as had been planned in the project budget. He discussed this with the engineer and found out that the soil where the drilling had been done was much more porous than the Brazilian Reclamation Agency's bid specifications had indicated. The engineer expected that it would take double the concrete and labor planned in order to construct a powerhouse that met the requirements.

When Don and the manager met with the project manager, Don brought up the powerhouse problem. The manager agreed that it was a problem but said he expected to successfully negotiate an adjustment to the price of the contract to compensate for the additional costs. This became a major issue as the audit progressed, especially because a quick settlement with the Brazilian government was not forthcoming and the potential loss was material to Rineholt's financial statements. The final resolution was to provide for the loss in the financial statements. Rineholt management argued against recording the loss, but The Firm held to the position that it was not in conformity with GAAP to assume the contract would be successfully renegotiated. As it turned out, the loss was finally realized. The client was grateful that The Firm took a hard stand on the issue; if it hadn't, the SEC might have held management responsible for improper accounting. It was clear to everyone in the office that Don's vigilance was responsible for this outcome.

During my fifth year, I spent a good portion of my spare time working on my "plan" to become an effective business developer. I started by talking to the two people I thought could help me the most—my father and The Bear.

I called my dad and said I'd like to meet with him in his office to get some business advice. When he heard that it was about business development, he said that he also wanted me to talk to one of his partners, David Tisdale, who was on the audit committee of two Bay Area corporations.

When I met with Dad, he started off our conversation with a statement and an interesting question: "Business development in a professional firm is selling, Jack, and I think the most important thing is for you to know what it is that you're selling. Do you know?"

"Well, we sell services—audits, tax services, and consulting."

"Are you sure? I would have thought you were selling competence, objectivity, and reliability. That's what I sell as an attorney, and I don't see that being a CPA is different. When your clients call you, they have a problem. They want to use you as a sounding board. They want honest advice, but they want the advice to be competent. They also want to feel that whenever they do call on you, they can count on the fact that you'll deliver on your promises. I know that the *form* of your services is audits, tax, and consulting, but the *substance* is competence, objectivity, and reliability. If you can communicate that to your clients and potential clients, I think you'll do fine."

When Dad said this, it seemed obvious, but I hadn't really looked at our services in quite that way before.

My meeting with David Tisdale was equally enlightening. Tisdale told me that client relations were people relations and that understanding personalities was extremely important. He illustrated this with an interesting story.

"I'm on the audit committee of J. W. Ehrhardt, Jack. It's a large industrial cleaning service that cleans office and industrial buildings all over northern California. Ehrhardt decided to change auditors a couple of years ago, and the audit committee had to decide which new firm to engage. The company is run by old Joe Ehrhardt and his oldest son, Samuel. Joe decided to change auditors when the old firm changed audit partners two times in four years. Joe is a member of the old school, so to speak, and likes to know the people he does business with—he likes to be friends with them.

"Anyway, we got proposals from four large firms, yours included. We read the proposals and then had three of the firms come in to make an oral presentation to the audit committee, Joe, and Sam. We washed one firm out because the cost estimate in its written proposal was way out of line.

"The first firm that presented, which was your firm, did a nice job, but it built the presentation around a computer-assisted slide show and talked more about the firm's national capabilities than about who would be doing our work. Joe felt uncomfortable with this. He doesn't own a computer and never will. It was one generation talking to another, and the gap was a big one.

"The second firm came in without a slide show, but with a written document that emphasized the capabilities of the people for the job. It also contained some tentative recommendations for tax savings that were impressive. The presentation by the second firm was really more of a conversation. It was low-key, and the firm's proposed auditors were able to establish a real rapport with Joe. Even though the audit committee was making the decision, we weren't going to engage a firm Joe didn't like. He was the decision maker, and he liked this firm; so, this was the one we hired.

"We might have hired the third firm, but something happened during their oral presentation that really killed them. The person who would have been the manager on the job was relating that he knew a person who worked for the company. When he did this he said, and I quote, 'Oh yeah, *her and me* were friends in school.' That little display of poor grammar just turned all of us cold."

"Do you mean something like grammar can have that big an effect?" I asked.

"Oh yes. Grammar, dress, table manners, personal habits. Everything a professional does conveys a message about him or her as a person, and the client or potential client will transfer that message over to his or her perception of the job that person will do."

When I called Barnes for an appointment so that he could share his wisdom about business development with me, he said, "Sure. How about Saturday afternoon at the golf club? You can give me some advice on my swing. You corrected my hook, and now I'm starting to slice all the time."

So we played and talked. The Bear, as usual, was in a philosophical mood. "My belief, Jack, is that the best sources of business are the clients we already have. Every client is like an annuity for continuing work, and if our clients do well, they'll ask us to do more work for them as well. They'll also refer their friends to us and serve as references when we propose on new work. That all assumes, of course, that we do a good job for them."

"I've talked to my dad about his views on this, and that's what he emphasized—competence, objectivity, and reliability," I said.

"Your dad's a good attorney with an excellent firm. I think he's right on target. I'm sure you're well aware that I call every one of our audit clients, not just the ones I manage, at least once a year to find out how we're doing. You know, Jack, every contact a client has with us is either a good experience, a neutral experience, or a bad experience. My goal is to make sure that there are no bad ones and as many good ones as possible. In fact, I even have friends of mine call the office or come in from time to time and tell me how they reacted to the telephone operator and the receptionist.

"Clients are funny in some ways. They won't always complain about something they don't like; they'll just decide to change to another firm. Besides that, they'll tell others that they didn't like our performance. I know we spend a lot of time worrying about whether our fees are competitive, but I think clients are much more likely to leave us for perceived service problems than they are over fees. That means the partner and manager have to be out at the client's office making sure they know what the client's problems are and how well we are doing to help them. I've found that if we approach a client about the quality of our service and find out there is a problem, the client will give us a second chance if we resolve the problem quickly and effectively.

"I'll tell you another thing that is absolutely essential, Jack: If your client's CEO isn't calling on you for advice, you don't have an adequate client relationship. [Bearism No. 18.] It means you have been spending all your time with the financial people and not enough time with the real boss of the place, and it means you haven't demonstrated that you're a resource to the client as a problem solver. I know that some accountants feel uncomfortable with operating people, but that's something they have to get over in order to be successful in this business. And some partners are reluctant to spend too much time in the field because it adds cost to the job. But I'll tell you, Jack, you never really have trouble collecting for partner time. [Bearism No. 19.]

"Of course, a big problem is that even when we do a first-class job, we can still lose a client through a merger or an acquisition. That's why we have to add to our client base and help our clients find acquisitions to make, rather than be gobbled up by a bigger company."

After I talked to The Bear and my dad, I felt pretty comfortable moving ahead. First, I'd take a realistic look at my relationship with each of my clients. I wanted to make sure that I knew the CEO, or at least the highest-ranking operating officer that I had access to, and then I wanted to begin a program to get to know each of them as well as I could. I'd keep a file of notes on each of my client contacts, containing dates, events, and personal items. I would review these before a subsequent contact. I would also dust off my old networking file, and I would begin to implement the part of my plan that dealt with the construction industry.

My networking file of my college contacts was now five years old and sadly out of date. I took the file to the business school and reviewed it with Sally Philotakos, the Alumni Relations Director. Sally was able to give me current addresses and phone numbers for most of the people on my list. She also said that the Business Alumni Association was looking for new, young board members and asked me if I would like to be considered. I said that I would be interested, and she promised I would be asked to join the board.

After my visit with Sally, I began calling each person on my updated network list to ask if they would like to have lunch to "catch up on things." I received many good responses and began to have one or two lunches a week with my former college friends. I approached these lunches from the viewpoint of trying to find something *I* could do for *my guest,* to develop a quid pro quo. I figured if I could help someone else out, he or she would find a way to pay me back sometime in the future. I thought of it as my "Godfather" approach.

I hit it off particularly well with Hank Maskeller, who had gone on to law school and then become an associate with a firm that was a competitor of my father's. Hank had gone into corporate law and had met my father at bar association meetings. Hank also liked to play golf and remembered that I had been a hotshot golfer as a junior. We agreed to get together the following Saturday to play and then to have dinner with our wives in the evening. This led to continuing contact with Hank and Terry, and we all became good friends. Hank and I promised that we would try to send some clients each other's way when we could.

I kept a follow-up file on each one of my network contacts, just as I did for client contacts. It was work to maintain all these files, but I was convinced it was an effort that would pay off in the long run.

I did three things to enhance my expertise in the construction industry. First, I joined the Association of General Contractors and began attending monthly meetings. Before I joined, I visited each of my construction clients and told them that I was joining and that I would like to get more involved in industry activities. They were very supportive and introduced me to many of their friends in the industry.

The second thing I did was to have a conversation with each of my clients that went something like this:

"Ed [or John or Bill], I'd like to ask you a favor."

"Sure, Jack."

"I'm trying to get ahead in my firm, and that means I need to start bringing in new business. I feel that I've done a good job for you, and I wonder if you wouldn't mind putting in a good word for me with other contractors you know if it's ever convenient."

"Well, I'd be happy to."

As a result of this simple strategy, I obtained two new clients within the first year. And when I thanked the clients that made the referrals, they seemed as happy about it as I was. I realized that they were proud of their accountant and wanted to share in my success.

Finally, with regard to construction, I did some formal research and writing. Thinking back on my experience with Wilson Frazier, I wrote an article titled "Critical Success Factors for Residential Contractors." This turned out to be easier than I expected, and the article was published in a contractors' trade publication. Then I tackled a more ambitious project. One of the CSFs in my article was the ability to estimate jobs accurately. There was a lot of software available to contractors to do bidding and job accounting, but no comprehensive study of the software had ever been done. So, I did a study of the available software, judging what the strengths and weaknesses of each would be for contractors of various sizes and types. The result was a second article that was very well received. I was even asked to speak about it at the national Association of General Contractors meeting.

By the end of my fifth year, I had my business development "systems" working on all cylinders. My relationships with my clients were improving, I had brought in two new construction clients and was certain others would follow, and I was still receiving requests for statistical consultation. My major hope was that, sooner or later, I'd "hit a home run," which in business development parlance means bringing in a big new client.

Discussion Questions

10–1 *How important is it to understand one's own personal strengths and weaknesses in carrying out a career?*

10–2 *Do you agree with Jack's analysis of the requisite skills for long-term success in public accounting? And in other fields?*

10–3 *Is it wise to become an industry specialist? If so, how is that done?*

10–4 *What are the advantages and disadvantages of a temporary assignment in a firm's national office?*

10–5 *What are some of the administrative positions/tasks that must be done in a public accounting firm? What are the advantages and disadvantages of accepting responsibility for those positions?*

10–6 *What is the nature of competition among peers in a public accounting firm?*

10–7 *What are the "costs and benefits" of holding tight on a technical position against the client's wishes?*

10–8 *How important is business development to long-term success in public accounting, and why?*

10–9 *What do you think of Jack's business development ideas? What else might one do?*

11

The Big Hit

I got my big hit. It didn't happen until my seventh year with The Firm, and it was more like a double than a home run, or at least it seemed so at the time. I came into the office one morning and found a message waiting from Hank Maskeller. Hank had moved up in the ranks at his law firm and was handling most of the work on smaller security registrations. I returned Hank's call thinking that he might be looking for someone to lunch with.

"Hi, Hank, what's new?"

"Jack, how are you? I've got what I think will be good news for you."

"I can always use some good news. What is it?"

"I've got a client, Flight-Freight International. Ever heard of it?"

"I don't think so."

"Well, they're an air-freight forwarder that specializes in shipping electronic components and various types of scientific instruments. They know how to handle this stuff so that it is protected properly—you know, temperature, humidity, and other types of damage control. They charge higher rates for this type of handling, but it's essential to their customers. And, of course, they do more routine types of shipping as well."

"Do they own their own planes?" I asked.

"No, not yet, anyway. Only the really big boys do that. They contract for space on larger carriers and then they consolidate several of their shipments to a common destination. They get a lower rate from the carrier than the combined rate they charge to all of their customers to that destination. They make a profit on packing and then on shipping. They have their own trucks for pickup and delivery, so they make money on that, and they also charge for various other types of services like document preparation and expediting international shipments."

"It sounds like an interesting company."

"It is, Jack. And what makes it particularly interesting is that they have been growing like crazy and are getting ready to do an initial public offering. They've been using a local accounting firm for their work and their investment banker has suggested that they engage one of the big firms for the IPO. He thinks it will enhance their market value. Anyway, the company called us about potential new accountants. They wanted two names. I gave them yours and Other Firm. They asked me to call you about setting up an initial get-acquainted meeting. If that goes well, they'll want a formal proposal."

"This is good news, Hank. I can promise you we'll give this our best shot. Thanks for putting in a good word."

We did give the Flight-Freight proposal our best shot. We called our other offices that handled air-freight clients for advice and assistance. We analyzed FFI's financial reports and compared them with their competitors'. We visited FFI locations and familiarized ourselves with their operations. We met with FFI's top people and talked to them about their systems, accounting and tax problems, and what they were looking for from their accountants. And we talked to their attorneys, bankers, previous accountants, and other contacts about FFI's management, trying to get an understanding of their personalities and how their decision about new accountants would be made.

We perceived that the most important thing to the company was to continue to grow to the point where it would be a major player in the air-freight industry. Therefore, we decided to emphasize what we thought the company would need to do to maintain its rapid growth rate and what we could do to support it in achieving that goal. We committed the time of one of our firm's consultants in the New York office who had significant expertise in the air-freight industry. We committed an international tax partner from San Francisco to advise in that area. And we committed what we thought would be our best local-office team to manage the work on a day-to-day basis. The Bear would partner the job, and I would be the audit manager. There would be two experienced audit seniors assigned to the job—Len Trowbridge and Susan Mitchell—and Barbara Gillespie would handle the routine tax needs and coordinate with the international tax partner.

We packaged the proposal in a booklet that had FFI's corporate logo on the front cover. It included our analysis of the company, tentative recommendations about growth, a section on areas where we felt potential tax savings might exist, a detailed audit plan and fee estimate for the coming year, commentary on our role in the IPO, a biographical sketch on each person who would be assigned to the engagement, and general information about The Firm. We emphasized our expertise in FFI's industry but were also careful to make the point that because we didn't have any of FFI's competitors as clients of the Oakland office, the company was protected in terms of confidentiality. During our interviews with management, we had perceived that they were concerned about this.

We delivered our written proposal on March 28. The need to prepare it before our regular busy season was completely over was burdensome, but our team put in the necessary effort, and we were very optimistic about "winning" the FFI work. Soon after delivery, we got a call from Harold Matthews, FFI's chief financial officer, who told us that FFI was very impressed with our proposal. He indicated that our competitor, Other Firm, had also submitted a good proposal and that both firms were being asked to make a formal oral presentation to management and the board on April 10, at which time the final decision would be made.

Our intelligence about the company and our own impressions told us that there was really only one decision maker at FFI—Reston Smith, the chairman, CEO, and the company's largest shareholder. People we talked to described Smith as a strong-willed, hard-nosed businessman who had started FFI from scratch. I found him to be physically imposing, tall, dark, and handsome. He appeared to be soft-spoken and a good listener, but in the final analysis, he was insistent on having things his way. Apparently, he would delegate, but with a short leash, expecting his people to work hard and produce. We concluded that he would expect the same thing of us.

We therefore decided to make our oral pitch directly at Smith. Bear would lead, calling on the rest of us only to supplement what he would say or to answer specific questions. Bear would use a straightforward, no-nonsense approach. He would try to convey the notion that we were open, honest, and businesslike in our approach to our clients; that when we had something on our minds, we would communicate it directly without hesitation; and that when we were asked a question or given a problem, we would provide a quick and effective response.

Our strategy and our oral presentation went well and we were encouraged. There was one somewhat tense moment, but it was intentional, and it had an unexpected result. In our analysis of FFI's financial reports, we observed that the company's growth had given it cash-flow problems. Also, its attorneys and previous accountants had told us that the only real problem they had with FFI was slow payment of billings. Bear decided to try and nip that problem in the bud. He told Smith he knew that cash flow was a problem for FFI and that we would develop several specific recommendations to help the company with it; however, at the same time, he told Smith that we wouldn't take FFI as a client unless there was a clear understanding about timely payment of our billings.

In response to this, Smith was at first surprised and seemed perturbed. But then he laughed and said, "By God, Quentin, that's just what I would have said if I were in your shoes. I like your style and I like what you and your people have told us today. Thank you for coming, and thank you for being so honest with me."

We were all smiles during our drive back to the office, and for good reason. The FFI board and management met and called two hours later to tell us we were the new accountants.

FFI had a June 30 year end. Its plan was to complete the audit and file its registration statement with a full year's financial statements effective no later than July 31. This was a reasonably short deadline for us because FFI was a new client, which meant that we would have a lot of one-time planning and audit work to do, and that we would have to place significant reliance on internal controls. Based on our preparation for the proposal, it appeared that the company had reasonably good controls that would be made even better through the modifications to its computer system that it was presently implementing.

Our overall audit plan was to review and test controls and verify delivery equipment in May, to confirm receivables and test the allowance for uncollectible accounts as of May 31, and to test accounts payable and verify other asset, liability, equity, and operations accounts as of June 30. In addition to assuming good controls, we were assuming that the client would be able to give us its full cooperation in terms of access to people, schedule preparation, and computer time. We started our systems work on May 1, right after Len and Susan had both cleared their calendars. Although I had some other things going, I made sure I was available to them with a phone call and came by at least twice a week.

FFI's third-quarter balance sheet showed that about half of its assets were receivables from customers and that its largest liability was accounts payable to airlines and other carriers for the cost of customer shipments. Similarly, its primary revenues were from customer shipments, and its largest cost was for paying airlines and other carriers for those shipments. Supporting these accounts were two computerized systems: the revenue system and the cost system.

The primary document for shipping transactions is the air waybill, a standard form used throughout the industry. There would be an air waybill written by FFI for each customer making a shipment; then, there would be a "master" air waybill for the carrier used for the actual transport of customer shipments. Through the consolidation process, there would usually, but not always, be a number of customer shipments making up a single master air waybill. The matching of the revenue side with the cost side of each transaction was an important task for the company's systems to accomplish, so that all transactions could be recorded in the proper period and costs could be matched with revenues.

Transactions were initiated by customers at any one of FFI's company-owned offices or contracted agents. These receiving locations cut the company's air waybill for the shipment and delivered each day's shipments to the nearest FFI airport hub location. There, shipments were sorted by destination, consolidated, and shipped to common receiving airport hub locations. Individual shipments were then delivered per the customer's instructions. Data for the master air waybill were entered into the computer system at the hub locations. The company's computer system matched the related air waybill documents to ensure that all were properly entered and then updated the accounts receivable and accounts payable master files.

At the time FFI became our client, this operation was carried out using twenty-seven domestic and twelve international offices and four hub airport locations. The company's plan was to double in size each 18 months until it had full domestic and international coverage. Ultimately, it had plans for a fleet of one hundred planes and its own central processing facility, including its own airport in the United States. Its long-term plan was to be one of the three or four largest air-freight companies in the world.

In planning the audit, I decided to divide the company right down the middle and to give responsibility for all assets and related systems and transactions to Len and responsibility for all liabilities and related systems and transactions to Susan. They would share the responsibility for common aspects of the systems, and they would obtain help from Denny Mulavey, our office computer-auditing support person, in reviewing and testing the more complex aspects of the computer system and in using our generalized audit software program. I would review their work and jump in wherever necessary. I would also be responsible for a travel agency we found out the company owned.

In planning the work, I had to make key judgments about risk and materiality. The major risks facing the company that related most directly to the financial statements included changes in the economy and customer creditworthiness, and the impact of competition. The first two factors affected collectibility of accounts receivable, which was a major audit consideration. Competition meant that the company might have to make large, unexpected expenditures in order to remain competitive. The industry was marked by innovative uses of communication and data processing systems. The company was modifying its systems when we were engaged; these and any further expenditures could put a severe strain on the company's liquidity position. The other area of inherent risk for FFI that I was particularly concerned about was liabilities and whether all were recorded when they should be. My focus was on international shipments because of the possibility that foreign offices and agents weren't as disciplined as their domestic counterparts.

In terms of materiality, our preliminary analysis of FFI relative to the industry indicated that the company's profit margins were about normal. At the same time, the company was doing an IPO, becoming a public company. A lot of people would be buying stock in FFI based on our audited financial statements, and the statements would be scrutinized by the SEC. I decided it would be appropriate to set overall materiality at 3 percent of earnings before taxes. This was pretty conservative but seemed prudent. When The Bear reviewed the materiality number, he told me to change it somewhat. He felt that 5 percent was proper for planning audit tests, but he said we would take a very hard line on any possible adjustments we found. He also said that we would be conservative in specifying risks, particularly as this was a first audit for us.

We spent the first two weeks of May getting detailed systems and control descriptions from FFI's accounting personnel. Because we needed to describe these in some useful format for our permanent file, we decided to use flowcharts supplemented by narratives and sample documents for the major systems, and narratives only for other areas. Our plan was to review computer program controls, make observations of major systems aspects, including tracing a few transactions through the systems from start to finish, and to test computer edit controls by attempting to enter faulty transactions to ensure that they would be rejected. We would then perform additional detailed tests of those controls we felt were most important to our audit. We controlled our systems and control analysis with a matrix for each major transaction type showing control objectives matched with controls that were documented by our flowcharts and transactions.

This early stage of our work seemed to be going pretty well, until Susan came to me to report a conversation she had had with a clerk in the accounts payable section.

"Jack, I think we have a problem. When I asked Ms. Harmon whether she was having any particular problems with the airlines payable account, she said, 'Don't you know about the computer problem?' I told her I didn't, and she proceeded to tell me that they're having a terrible time with the linkage program that enters master air waybills in the payables master file based on entries of FFI air waybill information in the revenue/receivables master file. She said they found out on Monday that the payables master file is all botched up, and now they're trying to straighten it out. They've turned the linkage software off, and they're entering the master air waybills onto a separate master file by hand as they come in."

"Did she say when they'd have this straightened out?"

"She doesn't know. I suspect we need to talk to the computer people, but I didn't do that because Denny hasn't been in yet." Denny Mulavey, our computer-audit support person, was due in on May 20, a few days away.

Just then, Len walked in. "Hi, guys. What's up?" he asked.

"We've got a problem in payables," Susan answered.

"Well, I think we have one in receivables too," said Len. "As I understand it, air waybills are supposed to be paid within seven days under industry regulations. I know that part of competition in the industry is to be lax in enforcing the 7-day rule, but in just looking at a few transactions, I've found some unpaid air waybills that are *months* old. And when I asked for the aging summary, I was told there wasn't one. I think I'm starting to see why they've got a cash-flow problem. What do you think, Jack?"

"I think you're right. I don't understand why there's no aging summary; I saw one from last year in the previous auditor's working papers." They both gave me that 'What should we do now?' look.

"Okay, guys. I'll tell you what. Susan, you call Denny and make sure he will be here on the 20th. Tell him he may have to spend a lot more time here than we originally expected, and find out if that will be a problem. Then, why don't you begin the payroll tests. Len, you start testing the non-computer controls over shipments and cash receipts. I'll talk to Harold about the status of the systems modification and when they expect to have payables on line, and I'll find out about the aging."

"There's one more thing I'm worried about," said Susan. "The people I've been talking to seem really strung out. They're trying to process way more transactions than they can under normal circumstances. They're working four nights a week and Saturdays; I think growth is killing them. When I talked to Ms. Harmon about this, she said Matthews keeps telling her it will last for only a little while longer, but she expressed her doubts. If they don't get this cleaned up in the next week or two, I think things at year end will be a mess."

Harold Matthews, FFI's CFO, was forty-five years old. Before he joined FFI, he had gotten experience in both public accounting and in industry, having been controller of two other corporations, neither in the freight business. I would describe Harold as competent, but also intense, edgy, and somewhat obsessive. He seemingly tried to be helpful and patient with subordinates (and auditors), but at the same time, he seemed to wait for them to make a mistake so that he could demonstrate his superiority by revealing their error to them. In terms of my relationship with Harold, I often felt he resented me because I was apparently succeeding in public accounting where he had failed.

I met with Harold to talk to him about the systems project, handling the payables, and the accounts receivable aging. I framed my comments to him in terms of my overriding concern that anything that sidetracked or upset our audit plan might risk completing the IPO by July 31. Harold reacted very strongly to this.

"Good God, Jack," he almost shrieked, "there's no way we can slip past that date. That's just unacceptable. Reston won't stand for it."

"I don't have any intention of letting our audit slip, Harold, but we're on a tight schedule, and we have to have the information we need to do the work. If the accounts payable aren't on line soon, we'll have to find a different way to audit them. Can you give me a definite date for completion of the accounts payable system? And, I don't understand why there's no accounts receivable aging."

"We've had some delays with the systems project, but we're back on track. It *will* be finalized by the end of this month and the accounts payable master file will be clean by June 30. As far as the aging is concerned, we don't produce an aging summary each month; we do it only at year end for the auditors. Our regional salespeople get listings of overdue air waybills once a quarter and ride herd on customers who are slow payers."

"Aren't the salespeople motivated to increase sales volume?" I asked.

"Yes."

"Well, then, do you think they're the best people to oversee the collection process? I mean, if it's in their best interest to report high sales, they might sell to customers who aren't particularly creditworthy. And then they may hesitate to get hard-nosed with them about payment."

"Our emphasis is on sales," he replied. "That's what will make us meet our growth targets, not overconcern with our customers' ability to pay their freight bills. In fact, we don't think our credit policies are too liberal, and we think our regional salespeople are doing a great job."

"Okay, Harold. My problem is that I have to judge whether your allowance for uncollectible accounts is adequate. One way or another, I'll need an aging. In the meantime, we'll take a sample of sales and see what your collection flow looks like."

"I'm sorry, Jack, what do you mean by 'collection flow'?"

"What percent of invoices in each aging category is collected in the next month. We'll apply these percentages to each aging category at year end to make an estimate of how much we think the allowance should be."

"Fair enough," said Harold, "I'm sure you'll find that the allowance is fine."

I listened to Harold and understood him well enough, but I sure didn't feel confident that things would be as smooth as he promised. And then when I returned to our working area, Len greeted me with more bad news.

"Adele Cummings just called from Chicago, Jack." Adele was the auditor in our Chicago office who was performing procedures to verify the existence of delivery vehicles in the Chicago hub area. "She says she can't locate 10 percent of her sample of delivery vehicles. She doesn't know if the list we sent her is just wrong, or if the vehicles are really missing. She's worried that there could even be fraud and thought she'd better call us before she does anything more."

As I pondered this latest development, I suddenly realized something. I had spent my entire career as an auditor working on companies like Rineholt Industries and Frazier Manufacturing, companies that were basically well managed and financially sound. The audits of those companies went by the book. Yes, there were problems from time to time, but there were few surprises, and the problems were relatively easy to deal with. But FFI was a totally different story. Fundamentally, it was a mess, and I was right in the middle of it. Whether I'd be able to dig my way out successfully was the biggest question I'd had to face during my entire career.

Discussion Questions

11–1 *How is the problem of client confidentiality complicated when a firm or office of a firm audits more than one company in an industry, and how might this problem be handled?*

11–2 *What are the special things that have to be done on a first-time audit?*

11–3 *What do you think about The Firm's assessment of risks and materiality during audit planning for the FFI audit?*

11–4 *Why is timing so critical in an audit involving an IPO?*

11–5 *How is Jack's assessment of risk altered by the concerns that have arisen during the preliminary systems work?*

11–6 *What should Jack do about the possibility of delivery vehicles' being missing?*

12

The Rubber Meets the Road

A t 2:15 P.M. on July 22, The Bear and I drove from our office to FFI for a meeting with Harold Matthews and Reston Smith—we did not expect it to be a pleasant one. Smith had called the meeting because of my report to Harold stating that it was almost a certainty that we would not make the deadline for the July 31 IPO date. The main problem was that FFI had not completed its systems project to tie the creation of the accounts payable master file to its revenue/accounts receivable program in time to produce the year-end accounts payable trial balance. Instead, it had continued, and was still continuing, to key-enter master air waybills into the computer as they came into the headquarters office from the airlines and other carriers. We had taken a sample of FFI's late June air waybills and had used them as a control over receipt of carrier bills. We also had listed foreign agents and stations and had marked carrier bills against them as they were received. And finally, we had developed an analysis of the flow of carrier bills for April shipments received after April 30, keeping a running total of carrier bills received for June shipments by day beginning in July. All of these steps told us that it was unlikely we would receive a large enough portion of the pre–June 30 bills to know what the June 30 liability should be until well after July 31; in fact, we probably wouldn't know until sometime after August 31.

There were also two other serious problems that we didn't think Smith knew about. First, the allowance for uncollectible accounts was materially understated. While we were waiting for the year-end aging summary, we sampled air waybills in each aging category to see how long it took before payment was received. From this, we estimated a "transitional probability" for each aging category. For example, if an air waybill were 60 days old at the end of any month, there would be a 55 percent probability that it would be paid during the following month and a 45 percent probability that it would not be paid during the following month. For the air waybills in the oldest category, there also would be a probability that the bill was uncollectible and therefore needed to be written off.

With these probabilities, we would be able to take all the air waybills in each category and multiply them with the chain of probabilities over time to determine the percent that ultimately would be written off. This amount could then be compared with FFI's allowance to test its adequacy. When we made that test, it was clear that the allowance was significantly understated. When I discussed this problem with Harold Matthews, his reaction was that our transitional probabilities were overly conservative. I explained that we had based them on random samples, but he was not satisfied that we'd obtained reasonable results.

Finally, we had encountered a problem with the travel agency FFI owned. This was a "wholesale" agency that booked large tours. The agency would conceive a tour, make block arrangements with airlines, cruise lines, hotels, and other travel service providers, and sell the spaces to travelers. Their intent was to obtain discounted prices from providers based on volume and then to charge reasonably low fares to travelers. The agency also incurred significant advertising and promotion expenses to sell the tours.

The travel agency was located not in FFI's headquarters but in San Francisco. I decided that we would do the audit of the agency from Oakland rather than refer it to the San Francisco office. The agency was reasonably small, so I decided we would do all the audit work in July after the books were closed. The agency's year-end financial statements were completed on July 8 and forwarded to Harold for consolidation with FFI. Harold gave me a copy of the statements on July 9 and I gave them a quick review; they showed that the agency had a modest operating profit. I visited the agency along with Marilyn Bergman, a staff person, on July 11. We introduced ourselves to the agency personnel and got a tour of the place and an explanation of the operation. I went back to Oakland, and Marilyn stayed to begin the detailed work, which we expected would take only a few days.

The next afternoon, Marilyn called to tell me that the travel agency's operating profit was significantly overstated. It seems that two large tours were beginning in early July. The agency had billed its customers for the price of the tours and recorded the billings as revenues. Some of the costs of the tours had been incurred and recorded, but the majority of the costs had not yet been fully incurred; deposits had been made but were recorded as deferrals. Furthermore, the actual tours were yet to take place. The effect was a significant mismatch of revenues and costs, and the recognition of profit before the actual earnings process had taken place.

So, we were faced with the necessity of telling our client not only that his IPO would be delayed, but also that his expectations of earnings were significantly overstated.

Reston Smith greeted us cordially. He shook our hands and showed us into his nicely appointed office. Harold Matthews, who was seated in front of

Smith's large mahogany desk, rose as we came in. I expected Smith to seat us on the couches he had in his office, but instead he wanted us to join Harold at his desk. He seated himself in his leather chair and looked across at the three of us. After asking if we would like coffee, he got right to business.

"Quentin, I think you know me well enough by now to know that I'm fundamentally a problem solver. I place a great deal of trust in my people and give them a lot of latitude, but when they need my help, I step in and give it. That way, I think I help my people develop their abilities, and I spend my time on the more major things—the real problems—that have to be dealt with."

While I listened to this, I tried to watch Smith and The Bear as closely as I could. I expected this meeting to be a major client confrontation, and as much as I hoped it went our way, I also felt it would be an experience that would help me immensely in the future. It seemed to me that Smith was trying to come across as fair but tough so that when he reached the point of being demanding about his position, he would seem reasonable but also intimidating. That was my impression of how he dealt with his employees—some might call it a "velvet fist" approach. Bear, on the other hand, reminded me of a poker player. He smiled, didn't volunteer anything other than brief acknowledgment, and gave Smith his full attention. He looked as if he wanted Smith to think he would agree with everything Smith said.

"I know our timing for the IPO is awkward in many respects," Smith continued. "And, I know your crew has been working nights and weekends to get this thing done, and I really appreciate that." Smith looked at me as he said this, then he looked back at Bear. "Quentin, I think we're all on the same team on this, but Harold tells me there's a problem with our June 30 accounts payable that your people"—nodding at me—"believe will delay the IPO as much as a month or even longer."

At this point, I started to say something, but Smith leaned forward and raised his hand to stop me.

"I'm not pointing fingers, Jack. I just want to make two important points. First, any significant delay in the IPO date is unacceptable. I've said I'm going to make this happen, and I won't let anything stop me. Everyone's lined up and ready to go on July 31—the underwriters, the lawyers, and the printers, for God's sake. Any delay would be a disaster.

"The second thing is, I—*we* are asking only that you be reasonable about this. Harold has developed a solution to this problem that we believe you'll find acceptable. Harold?"

Harold cleared his throat and told us how he believed he could make a reasonable estimate of the June 30 accounts payable to carriers. "As you know," Harold proceeded, "there is a clear relationship between our air waybills and carrier master air waybills and other freight bills. The more business we do, the more we owe carriers, and vice versa. Fortunately," he grinned at the three of us, "there hasn't been any vice versa in some time.

Tying the cost side to revenue transactions was the whole idea behind our systems project.

"Anyway, as I thought about the problems caused by the systems delay, it occurred to me that we should be able to make a good estimate of the accounts payable by simply analyzing the historic relationship between revenues and costs and applying that relationship to revenues around year end. You should appreciate this, Jack; I had one of our systems people with a math background do a regression analysis between revenues and accounts payable. He came up with a formula for accounts payable at month end in relation to revenues for that month. I applied the formula as of June 30, and we've made an estimate of the accounts payable accrual on that basis."

Harold reached beneath his chair and came up smiling. "Here are our working papers for your review."

Smith got up from his chair, leaned forward and rested his weight on his extended arms, and said, "We think this should solve the problem, fellows. Jack, I understand you have a statistical background, and I'm sure that if anything is unclear, Harold can clear it up for you."

That's when The Bear finally entered into the conversation. He was no longer smiling. He straightened up and looked very serious. "Before we complete this issue of timing, Reston, I think there are a couple of other things we need to discuss."

"Oh? What are those?" Smith replied. He looked irritated that an obstacle had been thrown in his path, but he sat back in his chair.

"First of all, I want to make sure you know what happens when a company like yours issues stock under an IPO and something goes sour within a short, or even a not-so-short, time later. It goes like this: A firm of lawyers that pays people to watch stock prices and company announcements sees that your earnings drop unexpectedly. They take the position that the earnings drop was due to circumstances you knew of at the time of the IPO but kept to yourself in order to sustain an overly high share price. Then they sue you on that basis. And what's worse, from my point of view, is that they also sue my firm and me personally, on the basis that we should have found the cause during our audit.

"Now, I don't know how much of a chance of being sued you're willing to take, but I'm not willing to take any chance at all."

"Wait a minute, Quentin," Smith replied. "I'm not talking about anybody being sued."

"Yes, you are; you just don't know it. Your business has been growing by leaps and bounds. We think your volume is way ahead of your capacity to deal with it. Your accounting department is seriously understaffed. Things are getting messier and further behind by the week. Your people are overworked and tired out. We think your accounts receivable are reasonably accurate, but they're in terrible shape from a collectibility standpoint."

"What do you mean by that?" Smith started to look flustered and turned to Matthews. "What does he mean by that, Harold?"

Harold stuttered. "Well, Reston, Jack seems to think our allowance for uncollectibles may be understated. I think he's wrong. I was going to talk to Jack this evening about the problem. I didn't think you'd need to get involved with it."

I was getting into the spirit of things at this point. Bear was an inspiration. He gave me a look that said, *Go for it, Jack.*

"Let me explain, Reston," I began. "You see, this last year you've done a tremendous amount to broaden your customer base outside of your traditional businesses. I know you've emphasized the importance of that strategy to all your people and given bonuses to your regional salespeople based on expanded customer base. Your strategy has been very effective; your sales are way up over last year."

Smith looked at me as if he were wondering why this idiot was telling him something he already knew.

"There's a problem with this, though. I realize that air waybills are supposed to be paid in a short time after shipment, but your salespeople have gone easy on this requirement to get new customers. And, under your organizational structure, there's no formal credit function. Instead, regional sales managers are responsible for collection, but they're also responsible for sales growth. Do you see the conflict there?"

I reached into my briefcase. "Here, take a look at this aging summary. I've matched this year's percentages in each category to last year's. I know sales have grown, but look at how much older the average receivable is this year than last."

"Christ, Harold. Is this right? I didn't know we had slipped like this."

Harold looked down at his clasped hands, and I continued. "On this second worksheet, I've shown how collections flow over time in terms of percentages of each aging category that are collected in the next month. The final column shows the percentages that will never be collected and will have to be reserved or written off."

Smith asked, "What's the bottom line here, Jack?"

"I think there are two bottom lines. The first one is that based on your historical collection performance, the allowance for uncollectible accounts is understated by about $250,000. The second one is that we believe you could save a significant portion of that if you implemented a major credit system and collection campaign as soon as possible."

"Harold?" Smith said.

"I know we haven't been focusing on the collection side, Reston. And as I said, I think Jack's numbers are pessimistic. Specifically, I think the probabilities he used are wrong."

"As I've said, these probabilities are based on your actual data. They are based on random samples, but there's very little chance they're misstated by any great amount; in fact, they could be understated just as well as over-stated," I replied.

I was trying really hard not to be defensive at this point. Bear gave me a reassuring look.

Then Smith said, "But Harold, is the aging correct? It did come from our system, didn't it?"

"Yes, it did," Matthews replied.

"Well, the aging sure as hell shows a lot of old unpaid air waybills, doesn't it?"

Matthews just nodded.

"Then I'd say we have a problem," Smith said. "But how do we know your numbers for the allowance are right, Jack?"

"As I said, they're valid statistical estimates. Look, if you need more assurance, let me suggest this: You have some of your people take similar samples, and see if your results significantly differ from mine."

"Harold?"

"We can do that," Harold said, seeing a possible reprieve.

"Okay, do it," said Smith. "And draft a memo to the regional salespeople about collection. I think we include collections in the bonus formula along with sales, so that they get a bonus only for increased sales that actually turn into cash."

Smith then turned to Quentin. "So we have a *possible* understatement of the allowance."

"No, I'd say you have a *probable* understatement of the allowance that is a material amount. And there's one other problem—your travel agency."

"Our travel agency!" Smith looked very surprised.

"Yes. It seems that for the two tours set up for the beginning of July, your folks recorded all the revenues in operating income but not the costs. What they should do is defer the revenues and accrue the costs and then recognize them as the tours are conducted. I'm afraid after we book the adjustment, the agency will have a loss of about $150,000."

I thought Smith was going to have a coronary on the spot. He clenched his lips, the veins stood out on his forehead and neck, and his face turned red.

"Is there any doubt about this?" he asked.

"None whatsoever," Bear replied.

"That son-of-a-bitch," Smith said through gritted teeth.

"What?" asked the Bear.

"My brother-in-law. I bought that travel agency because my wife pleaded with me to do it so that her brother would have a job. He's been running it and he told me they were doing fine. Now you tell me he's been conning me all this time?"

Bear was consoling at this point. "I'm sorry I have to bring you such bad news."

Smith straightened up. "Okay, let's get back on track. You've told me that my earnings may be lower than we've been telling our underwriters. That will affect the price of the offering. Can you tell me exactly how much the earnings adjustment will be?"

I gave Smith a copy of a worksheet we had prepared showing the revised figures.

Bear said, "These numbers show no adjustment for accounts payable. We think it's very possible there is an underaccrual that will reduce income even further."

"So that brings us back to where we started, and your little speech about getting sued."

"Yes, it does," said Bear. "I appreciate Harold's attempt to estimate the accounts payable. The problem is that we have to *audit* it. In order to audit an estimate, there has to be some reasonable system in place to support your method of estimation, or we have to be able to make a satisfactory estimate of our own to compare with yours. Harold used regression estimation. Correct me if I'm wrong, Jack, but doesn't that have to be based on some stable set of data?"

"That's right," I replied. "It would also require at least thirty months of base data in a case like this, I would think. I'll sit down with Harold and take a close look at it, but I'm afraid it may not be a very reliable approach."

Smith didn't like this at all. He frowned and thought for a long moment. Then he looked up and continued.

"Quentin, are you telling me that there is no doubt in your mind that there will be a delay and a significant downward income adjustment, and that you refuse to go forward under any terms other than those you've given me here today?"

"Yes, I believe I am," said The Bear.

"Fair enough. I plan to do two things, then. First, I'll warn the people involved in the IPO that there could be a delay. Second, I'll call Eric Bogess over at Other Firm and ask him to consult with me on your opinion. I don't see this as any different from having a doctor tell me I have cancer; I want a second opinion."

"Sure, you're certainly entitled to do that. I'll be happy to give Eric any information he needs, as long as I don't get the feeling that you're using Other Firm to pressure me into doing something I know is against my better judgment. But there is another alternative."

"What's that?" Smith asked.

"Decide to hold off on the IPO, spend the next several months cleaning up some of your major systems and organizational problems, get your cash-flow problems under control, and then go public. I'm sure the offering will be more successful, and you'll be able to sleep better at night."

"I'll take that under advisement, Quentin. And, I assure you, I'm not trying to be heavy-handed by talking to Eric. Just prudent. I guess we are done now, at least for a while, aren't we, gentlemen?"

We were, so we left. On the drive back to the office, Bear brought up Smith's veiled threat about changing auditors. "You know, Jack," he said, "it's a hell of a lot better to lose a client than to make a decision that you worry may be wrong." [Bearism No. 20.]

Amen to that, I thought.

Harold oversaw continued sampling of the accounts receivable and was finally convinced that our numbers were reasonable. The company tried to get its regional sales managers to focus on collections, but, because they were salespeople by training and at heart, that strategy didn't work well. FFI finally hired regional credit managers to do the job. Harold wasn't convinced that his accounts payable estimation approach was faulty until August 12, when the carrier billings received exceeded his accrual and more bills were still coming in. Reston Smith consulted with Eric Bogess and his underwriters and lawyers and decided, on July 30, to postpone the company's IPO for at least six months. He also fired his brother-in-law. I have no idea how his wife felt about that.

From my standpoint, the FFI audit, and our meeting with Smith in particular, provided me with a great learning experience. It became clear to me that working on a messy audit like FFI, although trying in so many respects, was where the real learning about auditing takes place. One FFI is certainly worth many Rineholts and Fraziers in that respect. However, I wouldn't want to do FFIs all the time.

The final irony of the FFI audit took place in December. Smith called The Bear to tell him that he had decided not to go public but to sell the company to Airfreight Internationale, one of the "Big Four" companies in the industry. AI's auditors were Other Firm. It seems that after they had lost their chance to get FFI as a client in their head-to-head competition with us, they went to their client and pitched the idea of acquiring FFI. It was a good strategy, and it worked.

Discussion Questions

12–1 What special problems exist in the audit of a company filing for the issuance of stock to the public?

12–2 What unique accounting and auditing problems are present in FFI's industry?

12–3 What strategies might be considered for a difficult meeting with a client's CEO?

12–4 What concerns should an auditor have with regard to his or her client's "opinion shopping," and what are the related auditing standards?

13
Life Goes On

I awoke early on Tuesday, the morning following my partnership announcement, feeling great. I took time for a decent breakfast, and I got to the office before most others did. As soon as Marie arrived, I asked her to tell me when Don came in. She said he had left a message on her voicemail saying that he had decided not to come in until Thursday or possibly Friday. I wasn't overly concerned when she told me this. I assumed Don was spending enough time in Sacramento to determine how to join his father's practice. Actually, I was glad he wasn't coming right back if he hadn't yet resolved his situation in his own mind.

When I entered my office and looked at my desk, the euphoria of being made a partner began to evaporate. I had a stack of mail, a bunch of phone-mail and e-mail messages, and a "to do" list awaiting me that would sink a battleship. I realized that while taking an afternoon off to celebrate, no one had done my work for me. Furthermore, there were messages from Barnes and Bill Jepsen saying that although I was technically still a manager, I should consider that I have engagement partner responsibility for all of my clients, except for Rineholt and for one of Jepsen's big ones. The sum of all this was that I had a great deal of work to get done, so I started to prioritize it.

The first task I had to deal with was to respond to a problem one of my construction clients had referred to me. The company was a medium-sized contractor that had a controller plus an accounting staff of three people. The company's considerable growth during the past twelve months had put a lot of pressure on everybody. The controller argued that he needed an additional staff person, but the owner was reluctant to hire someone because he thought that volume might drop off and the company would become overstaffed. As a consequence, the controller and his staff were required to work a great deal of overtime in order to keep up. The owner observed that recently, the controller had been coming in late in the mornings, had been unable to respond to all his requests, and generally seemed "out of sorts." Finally, he discovered that the controller had missed the company's deadline for filing financial reports with its lending bank and that the reports filed had contained a number of errors. The owner asked me to assess the situation, to evaluate the controller, and to consider specifically how the accounting function should be organized and staffed.

I had approached this task by sitting down and discussing the matter with the controller, with whom I had always had a good relationship. In the initial visit, which took place on a morning about three weeks ago, we agreed on information items the controller would pull together for my review. The controller had been on time, but he looked tired and somewhat distracted. When I asked him how things were going, he indicated that everything was fine, but he wasn't very convincing.

The second meeting began at 2:00 in the afternoon. When I arrived at the client's office, the controller hadn't returned from lunch yet. When he got there at about 2:15, his face was flushed and he wouldn't look me in the eye. When he got close enough, I could tell by the smell on his breath that he had been drinking. This was not a new experience for me; one of my mother's brothers had been an alcoholic, whom the family had "dealt with" for years. At that point, I figured the best thing was to confront the controller about whether he had a drinking problem. Even though I did that as diplomatically as possible, he lost his temper and said he didn't have a drinking problem and that it wasn't any of my business anyway. I dropped the subject and went over the material he had prepared; it wasn't a very successful meeting.

This led me to call the construction company's owner and make an appointment to see him this morning. He was free at 9:00 A.M., so I went right over. I related my concerns to him about how my experience with his controller had always been positive until our recent meeting. I said that I was concerned that he may have started drinking heavily, and that he had been drinking during the daytime. The owner said that he, too, had been worried that alcohol was the problem, but that he had found it difficult to confront the controller on that basis.

As the owner talked, I began to get the feeling that his solution to the problem had been to get me involved. I told him I wasn't an expert on dealing with these kinds of problems, but that our firm had employed the services of a psychologist who was. I called my office and obtained the name and phone number of the psychologist for him. Then I told him that I thought we should defer making any major decisions about the company's accounting function until this personal problem was resolved, that we could provide temporary help with controllership duties, and that I would be glad to help in any other way I could.

The next problem of the day was to review working papers on my client Stay-Fast, Inc. StayFast was a manufacturer of small industrial fasteners, made to specifications for other manufacturers for use in their products. When I got to the client's office, the staff had the working papers pulled together, ready for my review. They all looked anxious to see if I would find that they had done a good job. I tried to joke with them to put them at ease, but my review was important to them and they still didn't seem to relax much.

Early in my career, when I started supervising others, I found that if I organized the job in a certain way, I received a great response from my subordinates. Basically what I tried to do was to give each person complete responsibility for some part of the audit. I found that if a staff person could plan the work for an area, including all the investigation and data gathering, and then carry the work out to reach a final conclusion, it was a lot more satisfying than doing one specialized task in several areas. So, for example, I would assign the review of the control system for purchases and disbursements and the audit of accounts payable to one staff person, and the review of the system for sales and cash receipts and the audit of receivables to another staff person. Each would be totally responsible for a whole area, understand it very well, and gain the sense of starting and finishing a major task.

I found that the work on the purchasing-cash disbursements-payables area had been done very well. As always, there were a few things that could be improved, and I made a few notes, but all in all, it was a first-rate job. I completed my review and went over my notes with the staff person who did the work, complimenting her on her progress. At this step, I always ask the staff person a few questions about the client's business and about possible recommendations we could make. I feel that understanding the client's business is the most important element of a successful audit; not only do I need that understanding, but the staff members who actually do the detailed testing need it as well. The purpose of this friendly little "test" is to ensure that that level of understanding does exist. This staff person demonstrated a good understanding of StayFast's business and had several good ideas for improving the company's controls.

My experience in reviewing the sales receipts–receivables work was disappointing. In testing controls, the staff person had taken a sample of sales documents for examination of several important attributes, including whether the quantity shipped on the invoice agreed with that on the bill of lading. The sample was a judgmental one of twenty items. For one of the items, there was a difference in the quantity shipped, accompanied by the explanation "checked with client—isolated error." Furthermore, when I got to the accounts receivable section of the papers, I found that the staff person had sent out mostly negative-form confirmation requests instead of the positive form indicated in the audit program.

I sat down with the staff person and discussed my concerns with him. First, I asked him how he had determined the sample size to use for the sales test. He said that he had used his judgment: Thirty items had been selected in the prior year, and he felt that by using twenty, he could save time and still do a good test. He pointed out that the audit program didn't specify the size of the test, and he was right. We were using The Firm's pre-printed standard program for manufacturing companies, with "fill in the blanks" for test sizes. I had been too busy to get over to StayFast to review the test sizes before the tests were done, so my concerns about sample size were really my own fault. Also, I believed that twenty items probably was an acceptable sample size, although I would have preferred thirty. I was critical that the staff person didn't consult with me before using twenty, but I acknowledged that perhaps, in giving him the responsibility, I should have made my rules of delegation more clear.

My bigger concern was that the staff person concluded that the error he found was "isolated." If the sample was indeed representative—twenty items out of several thousand—how could the error possibly be an isolated one? The staff person told me that a client person had told him that while upgrades were being made to the client's computer system, the program that matched sales invoices and bill of lading quantities was inoperable, and that this one simply "slipped through." The client person had "assured" him that there was no significant number of other such items. "How would the clerk know, and how do you know the clerk told you the truth?" I asked. The staff person hemmed and hawed, and I made my point: "There are no isolated errors in a sample. [Bearism No. 20.] A sample is by nature and design a representation of the population. You have to extrapolate from the sample to the population. So do that and come back to me with your results and conclusions about the sales system."

I also was concerned about the use of negative confirmations on the StayFast audit. One of the lessons that Wally Garner had beaten into me, and The Bear had repeated, is that you can't make an ineffective auditing procedure better simply by doing more of it. [Bearism No. 21.] Wally used the case of negative confirmations to teach this, telling us that they weren't particularly effective in reporting misstatements because a significant portion of customers might not read and respond to them conscientiously. I came away from that lesson believing that if there was any real chance of errors in the receivables, it was much better to use a smaller sample of positives rather than a larger sample of negatives. I expressed my concern to the staff person, who again pointed out that the pre-printed program gave him license to use his judgment—my fault again.

After I reviewed the StayFast work, I went back to the office to wrap up the day. When I arrived, Marie told me that Terry Davis had called from Bettis Construction with an "emergency." I called Terry and he related to me that Bettis was having difficulty completing the quarterly financial statements it was required to file with its bonding company. Bettis is a small construction company that builds residential homes to customer specifications on the customer's property. A few years ago, it had accepted a piece of land as payment for some work it had done. Bettis held the land over the period to the present and, according to Terry, had recently sold it for a significant gain. However, in making the sale, Bettis took a sizeable note and promised to make some improvements to the land in the form of drainage. These improvements were to be completed over the next sixty days. Terry stated that he knew there were some accounting rules that governed sales of real estate, and he wanted to know if Bettis could recognize the profit on the land sale in the quarterly financial statements.

I told Terry that Bettis could recognize the gain if it had a valid contract executed prior to quarter end and got a significant enough cash down payment from the buyer. I told him that Bettis would have to allocate the purchase price between the land itself and the improvements to be made, so that a portion of the profit would have to be deferred. Terry said he would fax me a copy of the contract that showed the terms of the down payment. I said that I would review it and call him back as soon as I could.

After talking with Terry, I turned my attention to getting my bills out. This was never one of my favorite tasks, but it was clear to me that maintaining a good, positive cash flow was one of the keys to running a professional services firm successfully. Putting it another way, anyone who got behind on billing his or her clients had to answer to The Bear in one of his "growliest" moods.

When setting billing rates, accounting firms can choose between two different philosophies. One is to set "standard" rates—the rate at which each person's hours spent on client matters is costed by the firm's accounting system—at a "floor" or minimum amount. Under this approach, the firm will always expect, under normal circumstances, to bill and collect this minimum amount. If the firm perceives that extra value has been generated in an engagement, a "writeup" can be taken in determining the actual amount billed. The client engagement partner and manager can be evaluated based on the total writeups they generate over time. The most popular alternative approach is to set standard billing rates at a "ceiling," the ceiling being the most the firm might expect to bill for one's time under the best of circumstances. Because these rates are actually billable only in a minority of cases, most billings include a "writedown," and partners and managers are evaluated based on their ability to minimize these downward billing adjustments.

There is a significant behavioral difference between these two approaches: The ceiling philosophy generally causes more pressure on partners and managers to maximize amounts billed. For this reason, The Firm had elected to use the ceiling approach, and I was always put in a position where I felt that I was squeezing every possible dollar out of each of my clients. Of course, this also caused me to make sure we gave them the best possible service in order to justify the size of the billing, and to keep very close tabs on the time that we spent.

The billings I had to get out now were all progress billings except one. Progress billings are monthly billings for work in process. When we meet with our clients to discuss engagements in the planning stage, we make sure we reach an understanding that we must receive progress payments throughout the period of the engagement. We simply explain that we have to meet our operating costs on a monthly basis and can't wait until engagements are complete to be paid. Our clients are businesspeople too, and they understand this. Sometimes we meet some resistance from clients who are having cash-flow problems of their own. On these occasions, we try to accommodate them to some extent, but overall, our philosophy is to shy away from clients who can't pay their bills.

The exception to my progress billings was one of my "problem children," Paul Moldine. Paul was a small residential contractor. We did an audit for him each year so that he would qualify for financing, and we did his tax work and some personal financial planning. Paul had entered into a joint venture with another contractor earlier in the year. They had purchased some land and were developing it jointly. The other contractor had run into financial difficulty, and Paul had taken over the entire project. His financial resources were stretched too thin because his former joint venture partner owed him money and because the size of the project had increased.

We had finished our audit of Paul's financial statements a few weeks before. Paul had called me with the proposition that if we would carry him until the development reached the point of providing significant positive cash flow, he would pay our full bill at standard rates—he had always been able to convince us to take writedowns in the past. I had to decide whether I should recommend to Barnes that we do this or that we "play hardball" with Paul. Paul had always been a good client, and if he were successful in completing the development, he would continue to be a good client in the future. On the other hand, he was effectively asking us to share in the risk of his project. Of course, if we did insist on immediate payment, he could tell us he wouldn't pay anyway, and then we would be confronted with going along with him or filing suit against him for payment—something we generally didn't like to do.

After thinking about this, I decided to recommend that we accept Paul's terms. I drafted the billing and took it over to Barnes's office for his approval. But time had slipped away from me, and both Barnes and Madeline were gone for the day. I added a note, asking Madeline to give the draft billing to Barnes in the morning, and left it on her desk. I phoned Libby to tell her I was on my way home, and then I called it a day.

Discussion Questions

13–1 Should an auditor get involved in dealing with the client personnel's personal problems, and how should Jack have handled the situation with his client's possibly alcoholic controller differently?

13–2 How does the workpaper review process work, and how effective is it in ensuring that a quality audit has been performed?

13–3 Is it possible to find an "isolated error" in an audit sample?

13–4 What are the strengths and weaknesses of positive and negative confirmations, and when should each be used or avoided?

13–5 How should Jack have "contracted" with the staff on the StayFast audit regarding delegation?

13–6 Was Jack's advice to Terry Davis correct? What FASB pronouncement would relate to this situation?

13–7 Which do you think is better, the floor or ceiling approach to billing clients? Why?

13–8 How would you have handled the billing to Paul Moldine?

14

The Unexpected Happens

Wednesday turned out to be a pretty routine day. I received more e-mail messages and telephone calls from friends and acquaintances from around the firm congratulating me on my promotion. I attended to the rest of my billings, did some other administrative work, and held a planning meeting for the interim phase of the upcoming year's work on Rineholt. I assumed that I would be the number-two partner on the engagement, behind The Bear. This meant that I would be responsible for the more time-consuming aspects of the audit: overseeing the audit work on most of the larger divisions and subsidiaries and the consolidation, and drafting the financial statements. Bear would be responsible for client relations and dealing with the tougher technical and client issues. No matter how many of us were assigned to the engagement or what our titles and responsibilities were, in the eyes of Rineholt's chairman and CEO, Quentin Barnes was The Firm. When major problems arose, he was the person who got the call and who made sure that The Firm responded.

I got home reasonably early Wednesday evening, and I didn't bring a briefcase full of workpapers or reading home with me. Libby and I played a game with the kids and put them to bed. We then went over our plans for a vacation trip to Hawaii that we had promised ourselves in the event I was promoted to partner. Libby said she was really beginning to like this idea of being married to a partner in The Firm. We went to bed, watched the evening news, and were fast asleep by 11 o'clock.

It seemed that I was having a funny dream, with some far-off noise distracting me from whatever it was that I was doing. I slowly came to the realization that the phone was ringing. I reached over and turned on the bedside lamp and reached for the phone. I glanced at the clock radio and saw that it was a little after 1:00 A.M. A sense of alarm struck me—late-night telephone calls usually meant bad news.

"Hello," I said, anxious to learn who it was.

"Jack, its Bill Jepsen." I felt relieved. My father was getting older, and I had developed a mild phobia that my mother would call one day to tell me his health had failed.

I looked over at Libby, who was now fully awake, put my hand over the mouthpiece, and whispered "Bill Jepsen." She look annoyed at first, but then relieved.

"Hi, Bill, what's up?" I said.

"It's Quentin, Jack, he's had a heart attack."

"Oh, my God," was all I could say. This was a shock. I couldn't remember Quentin Barnes ever missing a day of work from a cold, let alone something as serious as this. He was the strength we all drew from when we were under pressure or just tired out. How could he not be that way forever?

"Yeah, I know. That's the same reaction I had," Bill said.

"How bad is it?"

"It's hard to say. Sally called me about an hour ago. They had gone to their club for dinner and stayed to play bridge. After they went to bed, Quentin started having some discomfort. He thought it was indigestion and took some medication, but it kept getting worse. Sally called the paramedics about eleven and they took him to Memorial. He's in intensive care and stable; we'll all know a lot more tomorrow. I'm calling everybody in the management group to tell them to meet in the conference room at noon. Is that a problem for you?"

"No. I have a client meeting in the morning, but I had planned to be in at noon. Is there anything I can do to help out now?"

"No." Bill got very serious. "Just say a prayer for Quentin, and get a good night's rest if you can." And he hung up.

"What is it, honey?" Libby asked.

"It's Quentin Barnes. He's had a heart attack." As I explained to her what I knew, I realized how saddened I was. I had two fathers, and one of them could leave me sooner than I was prepared to accept.

There were eleven of us in the conference room for our noontime meeting: Bill Jepsen, me, and three other managers from audit; Roy Shantz, Barbara Gillespie, and two other managers from tax; and Madeline Stovall and Harry Anderson, our office manager. Don was the only member of the management group not there. The mood was pretty somber. Bill started by saying that things weren't as bad as we might have thought. Rather than a major heart attack, Quentin's had been "moderate," whatever that means. It appeared that he did not need to have surgery, at least not immediately; nonetheless, he would be in the hospital for a few days while the doctors conducted some diagnostic tests. Sally was going to try to call us in the conference room with an update.

The crisis of Quentin Barnes's heart attack really brought out the best in Bill Jepsen. Bill was 55 years old, two years from The Firm's voluntary retirement age and five from the mandatory retirement age. He had always been a likeable, easygoing type, firm when necessary, but never overly assertive. He liked to talk much more about fishing and basketball than about business. His clients liked him; in fact, now that I think about it, everyone did. Bill dealt with pressure by standing back, looking for the essentials in the situation, and organizing a solution. He was a great believer in goals and "to do" lists.

Bill must have been up all night preparing for the meeting. Madeline handed out a typed dossier that spelled out in detail what Barnes's responsibilities were and how they would be fulfilled in his absence. Bill would serve as partner in charge of the office. He would push more responsibility on his jobs to his managers and give partnership responsibility for several of his jobs to me. Each of Barnes's clients was assigned to one of the partners, including me. I would become the partner *pro tem* in charge of the entire Rineholt engagement. Although I knew I could handle the responsibility, I did hope nothing major came up before Barnes returned. The managers on Barnes's jobs would handle all routine matters and seek approval only when they thought necessary, or when firm policy required it. Higher-level decisions would be referred to Bill, and Bill would defer to our regional partner when he believed it was necessary. The one thing we *wouldn't* do was bother Quentin Barnes.

The phone rang at about twelve-thirty; it was Sally calling from the hospital. Bill talked with her for a few moments and then hung up. Bill told us that Quentin was doing fine and that surgery was definitely not indicated. Quentin would be in the hospital for the next four or five days and then at home for at least a month. He would be on a continued medication, diet, and exercise program. Bill said Sally had told him very firmly that she was not going to let Quentin "die at his desk." Finally, Bill said he was going to visit Quentin later in the afternoon, but that Quentin would prefer not to have general visitors in the hospital; rather, he'd have everybody over for a visit after he had gone home. Bill ended the meeting by saying, "Okay, everybody, let's get to work. I know you all feel the same way about Quentin as I do. The best thing we can do for him is to make sure everything runs as smoothly as possible around here while he's recuperating."

As we left the conference room, I glanced over at Madeline. She smiled at me and wiped some tears from her eye at the same time.

On Thursday morning, I got a call from The Bear. My first thought was that his voice sounded strong. Some of the fear I had built up about the future vanished when I heard it.

"How are you doing, Jack?" he asked.

"Wrong person asking the right question," I replied. "How are *you* doing?"

"Pretty well. I'll go home Sunday afternoon, but I'll have to take it easy. I wanted to talk with you about a couple of things. Could you come over here and see me about four?"

"Well, I don't know, Quentin. We all agreed we wouldn't harass you for at least a couple more days. Isn't it something that could wait?"

"It could, but I don't want it to. I promise I won't tire myself out. And, I got Sally's permission," he chuckled.

"I'll see you at four. Can I bring you anything?"

"Lord, no," he replied. "This place looks like a hothouse and a candy factory now."

I arrived at the hospital a little before four and found Bear's room. It was a private room, the door was open, and Sally was sitting next to the bed reading aloud items from the newspaper. Bear was sitting up in his bed with his head at an angle so that he could see out the window in case anything interesting passed by. His color was good and his facial muscles looked firm. If he hadn't had an IV tube going into his left arm, I wouldn't have known he was ill. I gave a light knock and they both turned toward me and smiled. Sally got up and greeted me with a hug, asked how Libby and the kids were doing, and then left the room, saying that she was going down to the coffee shop so that we "boys" could talk.

"You're looking awfully good, Bear," I said. "Are you sure this isn't just your way of getting in some extra vacation?"

Bear smiled and replied, "It's no vacation so far, Jack, but it looks like it may turn into one. The doctor says I've got to change my ways: no more 60-hour weeks, no more living on coffee and doughnuts, and no more sitting around getting zero exercise. As soon as I get out of here, I start on their heart recovery program. I'll have a dietician and a personal trainer, along with regular checkups from the doctor. He says that if I toe the line, I'll be fine; if I don't, I'm high-risk and I'll be in for trouble.

"But worse than that," he grinned, "he said all of this in front of Sally. Did you see how she was sitting next to the bed? Her mission in life now is to protect me from myself and all the other dangers in life."

"Yeah. You're a lucky guy, aren't you?"

"Yes, I am, Jack. Before this happened, Sally and I started discussing my retirement plans, and we had decided that I would work for two more years. My heart attack has made it clear to both of us that it doesn't make any sense to put off retiring any longer. I'll take the next few weeks off, and then I'll come back to the office and spend just enough time to turn my clients and my office responsibilities over to Bill, and to you."

When he said this, he stopped talking and stared at me with a smile on his face. It took me a moment to realize exactly what he was saying—I wasn't sure I really understood him or could believe him.

"What do you mean, Bear?" I asked.

"Just what I said. Look, Jack, Bill is 55 and has absolutely no aspirations to become partner-in-charge of the office whatsoever. Roy just isn't the type. That means we either have to bring someone in from another office or give you or Barbara the responsibility. When I counseled Barbara, she indicated that her longer-term goal was to head up the tax department, but not an office. That leaves you. Would you like to run the Oakland office?"

"Of course I would." I kind of blurted this out without really thinking. "But I don't think I'm ready for it. Do you?"

"Probably not this five minutes, but you will be by the time it's required. Here's my plan. I come back to the office and begin to turn all the Rineholt work over to you. We meet with all the top Rineholt people and tell them that because of health reasons, this is my last year as engagement partner. I'll stay involved on the surface, but you'll run the job and be involved in all the top-level meetings and decisions. Then, you'll take it over completely next year.

"I'll probably come into the office about half time for at least the next nine months. While I'm there, I'll spend my time coaching you on taking over as partner in charge. By next year, when I officially retire, you should be plenty ready to take over the helm. And if you run into any problems, Bill can back you up."

"But if you leave, and I become PIC, we will be short-handed as far as client assignments are concerned, won't we?"

"Yes, and with Bill and Roy retiring in the next two or three years, succession is a real problem. The way I see it is that if Don is willing to wait around another year, he should be promoted. And, at least one of the other managers will make it. If we have to, we can transfer somebody in. But I don't want to bring in a new person to be PIC—I want that job to be yours."

"Have you heard from Don?" Bear asked.

"Not yet. He took a couple of days off. He should be back tomorrow."

"When he gets back, talk to him. Please don't say anything about your becoming PIC to anyone except Libby, and feel free to talk about it with Bill. But tell Don that it's likely I will be phasing out and a partner spot will open up, and that he has a good chance for it.

"I know this is a lot and that it's sudden, Jack. Think about it. Come and see me at home on Monday and tell me how you feel about it. If it's a go as far as you're concerned, then I'll call headquarters and put the thing in motion. We're entering into a new generation in The Firm, Jack, and you'll be seeing a lot of young partners like yourself get these kinds of assignments during the next few years. And Jack, don't think for a minute that I would consider you for this job if you didn't deserve it, or if I didn't think you could do it and do it well."

"Okay, Bear. I guess I have to say thanks. I thought you'd be resting, or, at most, thinking about your golf game. I can see that was a mistake."

"I *am* thinking about my golf game," he grinned. "If I can turn all my responsibilities over to you, I can play golf anytime I want."

We both smiled and I said, "I hope you'll let me play with you from time to time."

"You can count on it, Jack."

It was a poignant moment. "I'll see you on Monday, then," I said, and went on my way. I ran into Sally in the hall. She gave me another hug and thanked me for coming. At that point I began to feel bewildered. How long had Bear been planning this? I had planned to go back to the office but decided I'd better just go straight home.

When I walked into the house, I must have had a dour look on my face, because Libby asked me what was wrong. "You won't believe what happened to me this afternoon," I said, and I proceeded to tell her the whole story.

"My God, Jack. I never expected anything like this to happen. What are you going to do?"

"Right now, I'm still in a state of shock," I answered. "I'm just going to let it all settle in and then I'll really think about it. But, you know, Lib, this is an incredible opportunity. How can I possibly turn it down? It means I'll be one of The Firm's fast-track new partners. Hell, I could be a candidate for head of Accounting and Auditing, or even managing partner some day." As I said these things, my head began to swim.

"What does this mean to us personally?" Libby asked.

"More money, more prestige. More demands on our time. More stress, I imagine."

Libby then said, "I look at Sally and Quentin; they sure seem to enjoy their life. But then Quentin had this heart attack. Do you think it was caused by his job?"

"No, not really," I replied. "Guys like Quentin will work hard at whatever they do. They find the job; the job doesn't find them. Quentin has been happy in his job—it's a perfect match. You watch, when he's retired, he'll approach leisure the same way he approaches work."

"How about you, honey—is this job a perfect match for you too?" Libby brought up the real question I had been wrestling with. I paused a moment and let the answer settle in my mind.

"Yes, I think it is, Lib. I feel great about being made a partner, but I can't imagine just leveling off there. I'd like to continue to advance in the firm. I'm a goal-oriented person, and it's just natural for me to keep setting higher goals. When I achieve them, it gives me a feeling of satisfaction, but then I start thinking about my next goal. That's the way I am, and I don't think it would be healthy or right not to admit it to myself . . . and to you.

"And Libby," I continued, thinking I'd better get it all out at once, "whether I max out at partner in charge of the Oakland office or go further in The Firm than that, I won't have much of a chance if you don't want this for yourself too. I'm going to need your help and support. You've always been there for me, but the demands on you will get worse, not better."

I stood there with my hands resting on her shoulders, looking into her eyes, hoping she would reassure me. After a moment, she smiled and said, "You know, Jack, the fact is that I love the idea of being Mrs. Bigshot. We'll have a chance to entertain and travel, and we can give the kids some experiences they wouldn't otherwise have had. I think it's wonderful. But I do have some reservations. One is that you may not be able to spend as much time with the kids as you should. And, I guess I'm worried that we may have to move. As you said, if you do a good job as PIC in Oakland, The Firm will certainly want to transfer you."

"I worry about those things too," I replied. I promise you I'll keep the kids as my first priority. If we ever find ourselves in a position where you and the kids feel like you're being sacrificed, I'll walk away from it. I promise. And, I also promise that if and when the time for a possible move comes, we won't go unless we both feel it's the right thing to do."

On Friday morning, I went in early. Bill was already in his office, and I spent a half hour telling him about my meeting with Barnes and confirming a few things that needed to be done right away. I got the feeling from Bill that he sincerely supported my decision to become PIC over the next year. I then went to my office and started to work. Marie came in on time and brought me some messages and coffee. She was concerned about Quentin; I assured her that he was doing exceedingly well and said that she should input that into the office grapevine. A few minutes later, Madeline came in and told me that if there was anything I needed her to do, to just holler. She looked at me in a totally different way than she had in the past; I figured Barnes must have told her about my future status.

At 9:15, Don burst into my office, all smiles and grins. I returned his smile, leaned back in my chair, and said, "Man, I'd about given you up for lost. Where have you been?"

"Washington, D.C.," he replied.

"I thought you'd be in Sacramento, talking to your dad and your uncle."

"I thought about it, but I don't want to work for my family. I love them, but I figured if I worked with them every day, we'd get on each other's nerves. Besides, I have always prided myself in my independence, and I'd be giving that up."

"So what's in Washington, D.C., besides a bunch of politicians?"

"I interviewed for a position as senior staff member with the chief accountant's office at the SEC. It looks like a great job. I'd be working with standard-setters, dealing with really tough accounting problems, and helping to make policy. You know my strength has always been my technical skills. I'd be right in the middle of everything. The chief accountant is a great guy, and I like the other staff members. Washington is an exciting place to live. The money's not great, but it will do. I'm sure Dee Dee can find a good job there."

"You sound like you're ready to sign up." I said it more as a question than as a statement.

"I think I am. After I talked to The Bear and found out I didn't make the promotion list, I figured I'd better cool off a little. I knew about this position and had already submitted my name as sort of a hedge. I had the interview scheduled three weeks ago, and I was going to cancel it if I was promoted. By the way, how is Barnes doing? All I heard was that he's had a heart attack."

"He's doing fine, but he's going to have to ease off. I'm sure he'll retire soon. I know there will be another audit partner slot opening up next year, Don. If you stay with the firm, I'm sure you'll have first shot at it."

Don's face clouded over. I could tell that he was wondering whether he wanted to risk reexperiencing disappointment another time. I didn't blame him. If his bad feelings about promotion were a mirror of my good feelings, the decision would not be an easy one for him. On one hand, he had a new challenge that he was excited about waiting in the wings; on the other hand, he could battle away here for another year, making an emotional investment in partnership, but without knowing for certain whether he would succeed. I guess it just depended on how much becoming a partner in The Firm really meant to him, and how happy he truly believed he would be doing it. Only Don could know that.

After another couple of moments of thought, Don looked at me again and a grin broke over his face. "I think I'm going to Washington, Jack." He saw my disappointment. "Hey," he said, "don't look that way. You'll have a direct line into the SEC. Hell, I might become the next chief accountant. And whenever you, Libby, and the kids come to town, you'll have a free place to stay."

I really felt torn about this. I wanted Don to be happy, and to make this key decision for himself. But I didn't want my best friend to leave town. And, I realized, my goal had been to talk him into staying, and I had failed.

I went home that evening and eventually went to bed. What a week! And I wasn't officially a partner yet—I wouldn't sign the papers until next month. Were the rest of my weeks with The Firm going to be like this one? I was going to be a partner for another 25 or 30 years. Would I be up to it? When I finished my career and retired, would I look back on this week with approval or regret? These were the questions in my mind as I tried to go to sleep. Of course, the answers would be known only in the days, weeks, and months ahead. I dozed off, thinking that I was excited to find out how it would all turn out.

Discussion Questions

14–1 Is anyone "indispensable" in public accounting, or in any other business?

14–2 *How big a problem do you think succession is in public accounting: at the engagement level, at the partner level, and at the partner-in-charge level?*

14–3 *Do you think it is usual or unusual for a person like Jack to rise so quickly in a large public accounting firm?*

14–4 *Do you think a younger partner like Jack could manage an office successfully? What attributes must an effective office PIC possess to be successful?*

14–5 *Does Jack seem like an overly ambitious person to you? Do you think he is typical or atypical of people who become partners in CPA firms? Can one succeed in a large CPA firm without being relatively aggressive about his or her career?*

14–6 *Is it possible to have both a successful career and a healthy personal and family life? What are the tradeoffs? How can one manage it?*

14–7 *What are the pros and cons of Don's decision about whether he should stay with or leave The Firm? Did he make the right decision?*

14–8 *How do you feel about yourself and your career plans after reading this book?*

Appendix

BEARISMS

No. 1   Our clients are really two clients: the company that hires us and the public that is going to rely on its financial statements.

No. 2   Good audits are done by good auditors.

No. 3   The way to get ahead in public accounting is to focus on what you're doing at the moment and to do it as well as you can.

No. 4   Always tackle the toughest problems first.

No. 5   Don't try to be the Lone Ranger.

No. 6   Don't be defensive—you come across badly and you won't learn.

No. 7   If you don't feel that you're in over your head, you aren't making sufficient progress.

No. 8   You never really know what your ethics are until they're put to the test.

No. 9   You audit the business, not the books.

No. 10   Healthy skepticism means that if we aren't skeptical, we're risking our professional health.

No. 11   Don't audit by "conversation"—get evidence.

No. 12   Always put things to the "reasonableness test."

No. 13   Once the fee has been agreed upon with the client, forget it and make sure you do a good audit.

No. 14   We pile a mountain of review on top of a pinhead of work, but we are basically relying on the competence and integrity of the staff.

No. 15   Time spent on planning and on-the-job training always pays off.

No. 16   Just because something was done a certain way last year doesn't mean that it was done right.

No. 17   When you delegate, make sure that the task has a beginning, a middle, and an end.

No. 18   If your client's CEO isn't calling on you for advice, you don't have an adequate client relationship.

No. 19   You never really have a problem collecting for partner time.

No. 20   It's better to lose a client than to make a decision that you worry may be wrong.

No. 21   There is no such thing as an "isolated error."

No. 22 Choosing the right audit procedure is what's important; you can't improve the wrong procedure by doing more of it.

Others, Not Illustrated

No. 23 The only proper way to solve an audit problem is to do more work, not to rationalize it away.

No. 24 A dishonest client will get the best of a good auditor almost every time.

DATE DUE